Origins of Analytical Philosophy

Michael Dummett

Duckworth

First published in 1993
Gerald Duckworth & Co. Ltd.
The Old Piano Factory
48 Hoxton Square, London N1 6PB
Tel: 071 729 5986
Fax: 071 729 0015

A catalogue record for this book is available
from the British Library

 ISBN 0 7156 2484 9

Photoset in North Wales by
Derek Doyle & Associates, Mold, Clwyd
Printed in Great Britain by
Redwood Books, Trowbridge, Wiltshire

1000139848

Contents

To Joachim and Eva

Preface

This book is a revised version of a series of lectures I gave at the
University of Bologna in the spring of 1987; I regret to admit
that the lectures were given in English and not in Italian. I had
no idea, when I composed them, of turning these lectures into a
book, or even of publishing them at all. I was persuaded to
publish them by my friend and former student Professor Eva
Picardi, of the University of Bologna; they accordingly
appeared, exactly as delivered, in two successive numbers of
the journal *Lingua e Stile*.[1] Later, Dr. Joachim Schulte, also a
friend of many years' standing, proposed to translate them
with a view to bringing them out as a small book. I welcomed
the idea: I had not intended to write a book, but the thought of
publishing a *short* book on philosophy, which I should never
have achieved if I had set out to write one, attracted me
greatly. Schulte made an impeccable translation, and added
the transcript of an interview between him and me conducted
in October 1987; the book was published by Suhrkamp under
the title *Ursprünge der analytischen Philosophie* in 1988.
There was later an Italian translation by Eva Picardi,
published by il Mulino in 1990, without the interview, under
the title *Alle origine della filosofia analitica*, and a French
translation by Marie-Anne Lescourret, published by Galli-
mard in 1991, with the interview, under the title *Les origines
de la philosophie analytique*. I take this opportunity to thank
all three of my translators for the care with which they
undertook this often insufficiently appreciated work and the
success with which they accomplished it. I have never

[1] *Lingua e Stile*, Anno XXIII, 1988, pp. 3-49, 171-210.

vii

published a translation of anything, but I have occasionally made translations, for my own interest or for use in lectures or seminars, and I am well aware of the extreme difficulty of the task. In my view translators, who obviously perform an essential function, are hardly ever given the credit that is due to them. Usually their names appear only in small print, sometimes not even on the title-page; reviewers seldom mention them, except to complain. Very often, however, they merit applause; and that certainly applies, not only to the three who translated the present book, but to others who have translated other works of mine.

Thus, although the English text of these lectures has been available, it has not been published in an English-speaking country, nor in book form. I have for some time been wishing to bring it out in English; but I have wanted to make some revisions in the text before doing so, having been convinced that some sections called for improvement. I could not undertake such revision during the academic year 1988-9, when I devoted a year's sabbatical leave to producing *The Logical Basis of Metaphysics* and *Frege: Philosophy of Mathematics*. Since then, I was, until October of this year, engaged in teaching, among other things, and could find no time in which to accomplish the task. Having retired, I have now been able to carry it out.

The book does not purport to be a history; the absence of the article from the title is intended to indicate this. This is in part because, as explained in Chapter 1, I have tried to attend to those causal influences which appear to operate in the realm of ideas independently of who reads what or hears of what, but also because it makes no attempt to be comprehensive: I have left undiscussed the role of the British philosophers Russell and Moore in the genesis of analytical philosophy; I have also left the Vienna Circle virtually unmentioned, let alone the pragmatists. The book is intended, rather, as a series of philosophical reflections on the roots of the analytical tradition: observations any writer of a genuine history would have, to the extent that they are correct, to take into account. I hope that such a history will be written: it would be fascinating. But my aim has been far less ambitious, and my book very much shorter than a real history could possibly be.

It takes the shape that it does because of a realisation that had been growing on me for some years past that the roots of analytical philosophy go back a long way before there was such a school. What is more, they are the *same* roots as those of the phenomenological school, which appears to many the antithesis of analytical, or of what they think of as 'Anglo-American', philosophy. I understand that futile conferences, composed of British analytical philosophers and French phenomenologists in equal numbers, used to take place in the 1950s, in the hope of establishing communication; but it seems to me that communication is more likely to result from an effort on both sides to understand how their respective styles of philosophy originated from the work of those at one time quite close to one another, and certainly giving no appearance of founding divergent schools. The term 'Anglo-American' is a misnomer that does a great deal of harm. Not only does it have the vicious effect of encouraging those who would accept the label for their work to believe that they have no need to read, let alone to write in, any language but English, but it gives a wholly false impression of how analytical philosophy originated. Important as Russell and Moore both were, neither was the, or even *a*, source of analytical philosophy; and pragmatism was merely an interesting tributary that flowed into the mainstream of the analytical tradition. The sources of analytical philosophy were the writings of philosophers who wrote, principally or exclusively, in the German language; and this would have remained obvious to everyone had it not been for the plague of Nazism which drove so many German-speaking philosophers across the Atlantic.

My realisation of this has resulted from my painful and still highly incomplete retracing of the steps taken by the young Ryle, who began his career as the exponent of Husserl for British audiences and used to lecture on Bolzano, Brentano, Frege, Meinong and Husserl. It is a great pity that little of his knowledge of those authors was preserved in print, and, equally, that, as far as I can see, little that he learned from them survived into his later work; the topic least successfully treated, indeed least treated at all, in *The Concept of Mind* is that of intentionality.[2] My interest in Bolzano was a by-product of my work on Frege, whom in many respects he so signally anticipated; in the earlier drafts of *Frege: Philosophy of Mathematics* there were extended comparisons between Bolzano and Frege, of which little survived into the far sparer version that I eventually published. But it is to others that I owe my interest in Husserl: to David Bell, who has written a book about him which deserves to awaken interest in him among the British philosophical public,[3] and above all to Herman Philipse. Philipse visited Oxford in 1982 or '83 and lectured on Husserl, and I had the temerity to co-operate with him in giving a seminar on Husserl's *Logische Unter-suchungen* in Oxford in the summer of 1984.[4] I have also greatly profited from the critical notice of *Ursprünge der analytischen Philosophie* by Barry Smith,[5] as well as from the writings of Dagfinn Føllesdal, J. N. Mohanty and many others.

There is some overlap between sections of this book and my essay 'Thought and Perception: the Views of two Philosophical Innovators'.[6] The explanation is that, before being invited to lecture at Bologna, I had written an essay about twice the length of a journal article; when I received the invitation, I used it as a basis for the lectures, expanding it to three times its length by adding much new material. During this process,

[2] Gilbert Ryle, *The Concept of Mind*, London, 1949.

[3] D. Bell, *Husserl*, London and New York, 1990.

[4] See H. Philipse, 'The Concept of Intentionality: Husserl's Development from the Brentano Period to the *Logical Investigations*', *Philosophy Research Archives*, Vol. XII, 1986-7, pp. 293-328, for an excellent sample of his contributions to the seminar.

[5] 'On the Origins of Analytic Philosophy', *Grazer philosophische Studien*, Vol. 35, 1989, pp. 153-73.

[6] In D. Bell and N. Cooper (eds.), *The Analytic Tradition: Meaning, Thought, and Knowledge*, Oxford, 1990; reprinted in M. Dummett, *Frege and Other Philosophers*, Oxford, 1991.

I was asked by David Bell to contribute to the volume being edited by him and Neil Cooper. Explaining the circumstances, I asked permission to submit a reduced version of the original essay; Bell agreed, and I went back to that essay, this time cutting it down to half its length. Before the result was published, Bell persuaded me that I had not done justice to Brentano; I therefore expanded that section to a more subtle discussion. For this edition of the book, I have incorporated much of what I wrote about Brentano in the essay, being unable to do better now than I did then.

David Bell, John Skorupski and others have been for a little time co-operating on a long-term project of research into the origins of analytical philosophy; I hope that it will eventually result in a book tracing the stages of this tangled episode of intellectual history, an understanding of which I believe capable of bearing much fruit in an improved insight into the philosophical issues. It must in any case contribute to closing the absurd gulf that formerly opened up between 'Anglo-American' and 'Continental' philosophy, which many in the recent past have taken part in bridging. Philosophy, having no agreed methodology and hardly any incontrovertible triumphs, is peculiarly subject to schisms and sectarianism; but they do the subject only harm. I hope, too, that this book may serve in some degree to stimulate that interest in the philosophical past that I believe to be a precondition of mutual comprehension.

In the conflict between the analytical and phenomenological schools, one could be neutral only by regarding both as equally in error; such a book as this could therefore hardly be written from a neutral standpoint. This one has been written by a practitioner of analytical philosophy. Although I have been concerned to show how close were the founders of the two schools to each other at the beginning of the century, I could do no other than argue in favour of the analytical side on points where they diverged. A book covering the same gound, written from a phenomenological standpoint, would be a counterweight of the highest interest: I hope that someone will write it.

Oxford, December 1992   M.D.

CHAPTER 1

The History of Thinkers
and the History of Ideas

It is important to analytical philosophy that it understand its own history, seeing itself in the context of the general history of philosophy during the nineteenth and twentieth centuries: especially is this true at a time when it is undergoing profound changes. In what follows I shall try to explore the origins of analytical philosophy; but this will not be a genuine historical investigation, for two reasons.

First, I shall ignore the contributions to the birth of analytical philosophy of the British philosophers Russell and Moore, and concentrate on those of philosophers writing in the German language. This is not because I do not think the contributions of Russell and Moore to be of profound importance, but because this ground has been fairly well worked over, and because, despite Russell's familiarity with the work of German-speaking philosophers, especially of Frege and Meinong, he and Moore sprang from a very different philosophical milieu. A grave historical distortion arises from a prevalent modern habit of speaking of analytical philosophy as "Anglo-American". Apart from its implicit dismissal of the work of modern Scandinavian philosophers, and of the more recent interest in analytical philosophy that has arisen in a great many other European countries, including Italy, Germany and Spain, this terminology utterly distorts the historical context in which analytical philosophy came to birth, in the light of which it would better be called

"Anglo-Austrian" than "Anglo-American". In central Europe, that is to say, in the great cultural region defined by the use of the German language for purposes of publication, there were throughout the nineteenth century a great many diverse currents in philosophy, which did not, however, flow along isolated channels, but collided with each other because of the communication between representatives of the different trends in the universities. More than one of these currents contributed, in the twentieth century, to the formation of analytical philosophy, which, before Hitler came to power, was to be viewed as more a central European than a British phenomenon. The shifting of the scientific and philosophical centre of gravity across the Atlantic, now seen in the United States as already accomplished, and, by anyone, as at least threatened, was, of course, principally a long-term effect of political events, that is, of the Nazi regime which drove so many to take refuge in America: the process is now being completed by those many contemporary European governments that have set themselves to inflict the maximum damage on their countries' university systems. That, of course, does not make it any the less real; but it is a grave mistake to project present realities back into a past in which they were as yet unimaginable.

It is not merely that I shall concentrate on only one of the two strands which went to form analytical philosophy: I shall scarcely be concerned to respect historical causation at all. A genuine historical enquiry must offer evidence that influences were transmitted from particular philosophers to other particular philosophers. To establish this, dates of publication must be scrutinised, diaries and personal correspondence studied, even library catalogues examined to discover what specific individuals read or might have read. I shall be unconcerned with any of this, and therefore mine is not a genuine historical enquiry, at least not one of the usual sort.

The history of ideas is full of developments that cannot be explained by historical enquiries of the usual sort. Someone advances a new idea and supports it with certain arguments; only a short time later someone else puts forward the very same idea, supporting it with very similar arguments: and yet it appears that he had had no opportunity to read the work of the one who anticipated him. Or, yet more remarkable, someone reacts against, or puts forward arguments to counter, that new idea, although, again, it proves that he had no knowledge that it had actually been advanced by anyone. Ideas, as it is said, are "in the air". The true explanation is presumably that, at a certain stage in the history of any subject, ideas become visible, though only to those with keen mental eyesight, that not even those with the sharpest vision could have perceived at an earlier stage. If we are interested in the history of thought rather than of thinkers, it is these developments that will concern us, rather than those discoverable by the processes of genuine historical enquiry. At any rate, it is these with which I shall be concerned: I shall talk about the directions in which various philosophical ideas led and what were legitimate developments from them, without much troubling myself about who read whose work or whether X derived a certain idea from Y or arrived at it independently. I am not depreciating genuine historical enquiry, which serves to satisfy a perfectly reasonable type of curiosity: I am simply engaging in a different, though allied, discussion.

CHAPTER 2

The Linguistic Turn

[handwritten margin note: Thought understood through examination of language]

What distinguishes analytical philosophy, in its diverse manifestations, from other schools is the belief, first, that a philosophical account of thought can be attained through a philosophical account of language, and, secondly, that a comprehensive account can only be so attained. Widely as they differed from one another, the logical positivists, Wittgenstein in all phases of his career, Oxford 'ordinary language' philosophy and post-Carnapian philosophy in the United States as represented by Quine and Davidson all adhered to these twin axioms. Some recent work in the analytical tradition has reversed this priority, in the order of explanation, of language over thought, holding that language can be explained only in terms of antecedently given notions of different types of thought, considered independently of their linguistic expression. A good example of this new trend is Gareth Evans's posthumous book,[1] which essays an account, independent of language, of what it is to think about an object in each of various ways, and then seeks to explain the different verbal means of effecting reference to an object in terms of these ways of thinking about it. On my characterisation, therefore, Evans was no longer an analytical philosopher. He was, indeed, squarely in the analytical tradition: the three pillars on which his book rests are Russell, Moore and Frege. Yet it is only as belonging to this tradition – as adopting a certain philosophical style and as

[1] G. Evans, *The Varieties of Reference*, ed. J. McDowell, Oxford, 1982.

4

appealing to certain writers rather than to certain others – that he remains a member of the analytical school.

On this characterisation, therefore, analytical philosophy was born when the 'linguistic turn' was taken. This was not, of course, taken uniformly by any group of philosophers at any one time: but the first clear example known to me occurs in Frege's *Die Grundlagen der Arithmetik*[2] of 1884. At a crucial point in the book, Frege raises the Kantian question, "How are numbers given to us, granted that we have no idea or intuition of them?". His answer depends upon the celebrated context principle, which he had laid down in the Introduction as one of the fundamental methodological principles to be followed in the book. The context principle is, however, formulated as one governing an enquiry into language rather than into modes of thought. If it had been formulated in the latter way, it would have said that there is no such thing as thinking of an object save in the course of thinking something specific about it. Frege's answer to his Kantian question would in that case have been that numbers are given to us through our grasping whole thoughts concerning them: the investigation would then have proceeded by enquiring what is involved in grasping such thoughts. The context principle is not formulated in that way, however, but as the thesis that it is only in the context of a *sentence* that a *word* has meaning: the investigation therefore takes the form of asking how we can fix the senses of sentences containing terms for numbers. An epistemological enquiry (behind which lies an ontological one) is to be answered by a linguistic investigation.

No justification for the linguistic turn is offered in *Grundlagen*: it is simply taken, as being the most natural way of going about the philosophical enquiry. And yet, as his philosophy developed, Frege became more and more insistent that thoughts, and not the sentences that express them, formed his true subject-matter. Natural language came to appear to him more of an obstacle than a guide in logical and

[2] Gottlob Frege, *Die Grundlagen der Arithmetik*, Breslau, 1884; bilingual edn., *The Foundations of Arithmetic*, with German and English on facing pages, trans. J. L. Austin, second revised edn., Oxford, 1978. See §62.

philosophical enquiries. Especially was this so after his realisation that he had after all no satisfactory solution to Russell's paradox, and that therefore he had failed in what he had set himself as his life's work, to set number theory and analysis on indisputably firm foundations. This occurred in August 1906; and he thereafter rejected his whole former conception of logical objects, including classes (extensions of concepts), blaming language for the illusion of their existence generated by the possibility of forming apparent singular terms of the form "the extension of the concept F". Thus, in November 1906 he wrote to Husserl that "The main task of the logician consists in liberation from language",[3] and in the article 'Erkenntnisquellen', completed in the last year of his life, he said that "a great part of the work of the philosopher consists in ... a struggle with language".[4]

Had the linguistic turn taken in *Grundlagen* been an aberration, then? Had Frege inadvertently anticipated analytical philosophy, but subsequently set himself upon another path? Such a diagnosis is superficial. After all, while it is in the writings of his late period (mid-1906 until his death) that we find the most vehement denunciations of natural language, it is also in the writings of that period that we find the greatest insistence on the mirroring of thoughts by sentences. "The sentence can be regarded as an image of the thought in that to the relation between the part and the whole within the thought there by and large corresponds the same relation between the part of the sentence and the sentence", Frege wrote in his notes for Darmstaedter.[5] Language may be a distorting mirror: but it is the only mirror that we have.

What above all renders the proposed diagnosis superficial is the presence in Frege's philosophy of deep currents driving towards the investigation of thoughts through the analysis of language. It is clear that he himself was not fully conscious of

---

[3] G. Frege, *Philosophical and Mathematical Correspondence*, trans. H. Kaal, ed. B. McGuinness, Oxford, 1980, p. 68.

[4] G. Frege, *Posthumous Writings*, trans. P. Long and R. White, Oxford, 1979, p. 270.

[5] Ibid., p. 255.

the thrust in this direction, which came from certain of his doctrines, but was impeded by others. In *Grundlagen* his attitude to language was as yet unperturbed by the ambivalent feelings towards it that he later developed; but the linguistic turn that occurred in that book faithfully represents the general tendency of his thinking, a tendency obscured but not obliterated by the reservations about reliance on linguistic forms that he later expressed.

I shall discuss three features of Frege's philosophy which made the linguistic turn a natural development from it, even though he never explicitly acknowledged that they had this character.

(1) The discernment of constituent senses as parts of a thought is parasitic upon the apprehension of the structure of the sentence expressing it. Frege claimed that the structure of a thought must be reflected in the structure of a sentence expressing it, and indeed that seems essential to the notion of *expressing* a thought, rather than merely encoding it. But, conversely, it is hard to explain what is meant by speaking of the structure of a thought without allusion to its verbal expression. I do not mean to suggest that the relevant notion of the structure of a sentence is attainable without consideration of its sense: on the contrary, the syntactic analysis must be carried out with an eye to subsequent semantic explanation of how the sentence is determined as true or false in accordance with its composition. The two notions, of the structure of the sentence and of the structure of the thought, must be developed together. But that is enough to overturn the conception of a study of the structure of thoughts carried out without reference to their linguistic expression. It does *not*, conversely, overthrow the conception of a study of language independently of a *direct* study of thoughts, considered as unmediated by language. The sentence expresses a thought in virtue of its having semantic properties, of being assessable by certain means as true or as false. The thought is grasped in grasping the semantic properties of the sentence: to speak of the structure of the thought is to speak of the semantic interrelation of the parts

of the sentence.

Especially is this true of Frege's leading idea of extracting a concept (in the pre-1890 sense of 'concept') by decomposition of a complete thought. The process was originally described in his *Begriffsschrift* as applied to a sentence:[6] but, as he remarked to Russell in a letter of July, 1902, "to the decomposition of the sentence there corresponds a decomposition of the thought".[7] No objection should be made to Frege's speaking of a decomposition of the thought: but it is highly dubious whether the notion can be explained save by reference to that of the sentence. For the process, as applied to the sentence, involves the selection, not only of a proper name occurring in it, but of particular occurrences of that name, and its replacement in those occurrences by some other term: it is quite unclear that any account could be given of 'occurrences' of the sense of a name within a thought that did not trade on the form of its linguistic expression.

(2) Frege held that it is the thought that is primarily said to be true or false, the sentence being called true or false only in a derivative sense; and, since for Frege the reference of the sentence is its truth-value, this means that it is the sense of the sentence that primarily has the reference, and the sentence only derivatively. He laid little emphasis on the generalisation of this principle to all expressions, but he did acknowledge it as correct: hence, for example, it is the sense of a proper name that primarily refers to the object, rather than the proper name itself.

In practice, however, Frege never conformed to this order of priority when expounding the distinction between sense and reference. He never first introduces the notion of sense, subsequently explaining reference as a feature of senses: he speaks first of the *expression* as having reference, and proceeds either to argue that it also has a sense or to say something about what its sense consists in. This order of exposition is actually demanded by his conception of the sense

[6] G. Frege, *Begriffsschrift*, Halle, 1879, §§9-10; Eng. trans. by T. W. Bynum, *Conceptual Notation and related articles*, Oxford, 1972.
[7] G. Frege, *Philosophical and Mathematical Correspondence*, p. 142.

of an expression as the way in which its reference is given: for it follows from this conception that the notion of sense cannot be explained save by appeal to that of reference, and so we must first have the notion of reference. Now if we have the notion of reference before we have that of sense, we cannot construe reference as a property of the sense, but only of the expression. It follows that Frege's thesis that it is the sense to which the reference is primarily to be ascribed is incorrect.

This comes out very clearly in *Grundgesetze*,[8] Part I. Frege fixes the intended interpretation of his symbolism by stipulations which lay down what the *reference* of each expression, whether simple or compound, is to be: together, these stipulations determine under what conditions each formula has the value *true*. Sense has yet to be mentioned: so, if the notion of an expression's having a reference were derivative from that of a sense's having a corresponding reference, so that we could understand what it was for an expression to have a reference only in terms of the possession by its sense of some correlative property, those stipulations would be unintelligible. On the contrary, it is only after he has made the stipulations governing the references of symbolic expressions that Frege explains what the sense of such an expression is; and he explains it precisely by invoking the stipulations governing reference. The sense of a sentence of the symbolic language is to be the thought that the condition for it to have the value *true*, as provided by the stipulations concerning reference, is fulfilled, and the sense of any of its component expressions is to be the contribution that component makes to determining that condition.[9] Thus, contrary to Frege's official doctrine, we must know what it is for a *sentence* to be true before we can know what it is for it to express a thought, and we must know what it is for an

---

[8] G. Frege, *Grundgesetze der Arithmetik*, Vol. I, Jena, 1893, Vol. II, Jena, 1903, reprinted in one volume by Olms, 1966. Part I is wholly contained in Vol. I, and is translated by M. Furth in *The Basic Laws of Arithmetic*, Los Angeles, 1964.

[9] G. Frege, *Grundgesetze*, Vol. I, Part I, §32.

expression to have a reference before we can know what it is
for it to have a sense.

Frege believed it possible in principle to grasp a thought
otherwise than as expressed linguistically; but his account of
sense does not show *how* that is possible, that is, how a sense
can be grasped otherwise than as the sense *of* an expression to
which reference can be ascribed. The difficulty cannot be
resolved by saying that the reference might be ascribed
directly to the sense, since the sense has been explained as the
manner in which the reference is determined: for this
explanation to be intelligible, there must be something which
the reference is the reference of, and this can hardly be the
manner in which that reference is determined. Here is one of
several places in which Frege's general doctrines are in
tension with his more detailed explanations.

(3) For Frege, an expression simply *has* a sense: one who
uses it does not need to bear its sense in mind throughout the
process of employing it. The sense, considered in itself, is
objective, and hence capable of being grasped by different
minds. As is commonly observed, the objectivity of senses is
not enough to guarantee the objectivity of communication: for
this we need in addition a condition Frege hardly mentions,
namely that it be objective what sense is attached to each
expression. To explain this, we need an account of what it is for
a sense to be attached to an expression. This, though again
not explicitly discussed by Frege, obviously concerns what is
involved in a knowledge of a language: if we follow Frege's
explanation of sense in *Grundgesetze*, a knowledge of the
sense expressed by a word or phrase will consist in a grasp of
the contribution it makes to determining the condition under
which a sentence in which it occurs is true.

Frege held that we human beings have access to thoughts
only as expressed in language or symbolism. He conceived of
thoughts as intrinsically apt for linguistic expression: but he
did *not* think of them as intrinsically being the senses of the
sentences of any actual or hypothetical language. For this
reason, it was for him no contradiction to suppose beings who
grasp in their nakedness, that is, without linguistic clothing,

the same thoughts as we do.[10]

The conception of a grasp of naked thoughts is, as we have
seen, in tension with Frege's explanation of what the sense of
an expression consists in: it is hard to see how an account of
naked thoughts could be given parallel to the *Grundgesetze*
account of the thoughts expressed by symbolic sentences,
since there would be nothing to *be* true or false save the
thought itself, and nothing to make a contribution to
determining the condition for its truth save the constituent
senses. Now sense appears correlative to the grasp of sense: a
sense incapable of being grasped is a chimera; when we know
what it is to grasp a sense, we know what that sense is, and,
conversely, when we know what it is, we ought thereby to
know what is involved in grasping it. So, if Frege is right
about naked thoughts, we ought to be able to say what it
would be to grasp a thought in its nakedness, even if we
cannot do it: it is hard to see how the notion could be claimed
to be consistent if we could give no account of it.

Still, if *our* only access to thoughts is through their
linguistic expression, an account of what it is to grasp the
thought expressed by a sentence should be easier for us: and
this will in any case be needed if we are to explain how
thoughts can be expressed and communicated in language.
We thus arrive at the following position. Frege has an account
of what it is for a sentence to express a thought. Either a
parallel account of what constitutes a naked thought can be
arrived at by simply deleting the references to linguistic
items, or it cannot. If it can, then an account of thoughts,
independent of language, is easily derived from an account of
language. If it cannot, we have no account of thoughts save by
reference to language. In the former case, the first axiom of
analytical philosophy is established, but not the second: in the
latter case, both are established.

The question, "What confers on a sentence the sense which
it has?", may be answered, "The speaker's understanding it as
having that sense". The next question, "In what does their so

[10] G. Frege, 'Erkenntnisquellen', 1924-5, *Posthumous Writings*, p. 269.

understanding it consist?", may be answered, after the manner of Frege's *Grundgesetze* account, "In their regarding its truth-value as being determined in the appropriate way", or "In their taking the appropriate condition as being required to obtain for the sentence to be true". Frege's account of sense thus rests on the notion of truth: as he says in 'Der Gedanke', "thoughts stand in the closest connection with truth".[11] But now a further question arises: "What determines under what conditions a sentence is true?" What Frege fails to stress as heavily as that sense is bound up with truth is that the concept of truth is in its turn bound up with that of assertion. He does not wholly neglect this connection: in a remarkable unpublished fragment of 1915, he speaks of the word "true" as attempting, in vain, "to make the impossible possible, namely to make what corresponds to the assertoric force appear as a contribution to the thought".[12] For all that, the connection between truth and assertion was not a salient doctrine of Frege's: not one of those he reiterated with great emphasis in many different writings. It is, however, undeniable. It would be impossible to discover from specifications of the conditions under which the sentences of a language had the value *true* or the value *false*, but in which the two truth-values were designated only by the letters "A" and "B", which of "A" and "B" represented the value *true* and which the value *false*. To ascertain this, it would be necessary to know, for some sample sentences, with what significance speakers of the language invested assertoric utterances of it. Frege pointed out that we can have no reason to postulate a distinct linguistic act of denial alongside that of assertion:[13] but, equally, as Wittgenstein observed in the *Tractatus*, we cannot imagine a language whose speakers make denials, but no assertions.[14] A form of utterance employed to transmit information can only

[11] G. Frege, 'Der Gedanke', 1918, p. 74; Eng. trans. in G. Frege, *Collected Papers*, ed. B. McGuinness, Oxford, 1984, p. 368.
[12] G. Frege, *Posthumous Writings*, p. 252. See also 'Der Gedanke'.
[13] G. Frege, 'Die Verneinung', 1918; *Collected Papers*, pp. 373-89.
[14] Ludwig Wittgenstein, *Tractatus Logico-Philosophicus*, trans. C. K. Ogden, London, 1922; trans. D. Pears and B. McGuinness, London, 1961; 4.062.

be taken as carrying assertoric force: and a statement is true just in case an assertion of it is correct.

Frege's theory of sense and of reference makes no appeal to the social character of language: although he emphasises the communicability of sense, his account of what sense is could apply as well to the senses of the expressions of an idiolect as to those of the expressions of a common language. No such account could be given of force. Frege distinguished force from sense; but he offered no account of it. For him, it comprised assertoric and interrogative force; a smoother and more plausible theory is obtained if we add in imperatival and optative force (and doubtless other varieties), although Frege himself would not have admitted that the content of a command or of the expression of a wish can be taken to be a thought, like the content of an assertion or of a question to be answered "Yes" or "No". Even on Frege's narrower conception, however, force can hardly be conceived to exist save as attached to sentences uttered in the course of linguistic interchange. Having insisted on a sharp distinction between sense and force – between the thought expressed by a sentence and the force attached to an utterance of it – Frege was content to leave it at that, without attempting any more detailed account of any particular type of force. He did not even say whether, in his view, a non-circular account of what assertoric force consists in was or was not possible; he simply relied on his readers' pre-theoretical knowledge of what an assertion is. But his theory of sense cannot be seen as separable from the notion of assertoric force. The sentences of a langugage could not express the thoughts they do unless they, or related sentences, were capable of being uttered with assertoric force, that is, to make assertions; for it is only in virtue of their being so used that they may be said to have truth-conditions. In consequence of this, therefore, a study of the *use* of language in communication is a legitimate development of Frege's theory, indeed a necessary supplement to it.

These are some of the pointers in Frege's work to the need for the linguistic turn, pointers which Frege himself did not read wholly aright. They explain why his work came to be of such intense interest to analytical philosophers; why, indeed, he was the grandfather of analytical philosophy. He provided the first plausible account in the history of philosophy of what thoughts are and of what the meanings of sentences and their component words consist in. Those who found themselves driven to analyse thought by analysing linguistic meaning had no option but to build on the foundations he had laid.

CHAPTER 3

Truth and Meaning

One of the things that Frege saw is now a commonplace, namely that the concepts of meaning and truth are inextricably bound together. A failure to perceive this underlay the classical 'theories of truth', developed contemporaneously with Frege's work, theories like the correspondence theory and the coherence theory. Such theories considered meaning as given. They did not ask, "What, in general, renders (an utterance of) a *sentence* true?", but, "What, in general, renders a *proposition* true?". Here a proposition is what the utterance of a sentence *expresses*: to grasp the proposition, you must know what the sentence means. Hence, in asking the question, "What, in general, renders a proposition true?", we are presupposing that the meanings of sentences can be taken as given in advance of a knowledge of what renders them true or false. In the presence of such a presupposition, however, no non-trivial answer can be given to the question. Almost anything could be taken as rendering some sentence true: it depends on what the sentence *means*. In fact, it is by grasping what would render it true that we apprehend what it means. There can therefore be no illuminating account of the concept of truth which presupposes meaning as already given: we cannot be in the position of grasping meaning but as yet unaware of the condition for the truth of propositions. Truth and meaning can only be explained *together*, as part of a single theory.

Frege rejected the correspondence theory, on grounds that

would apply equally to any theory of truth similarly
conceived. It was luminously clear to him that the concept of
truth could not be posterior to a grasp of sense; and the
connection between truth and sense that Frege perceived was
explained with great clarity by Wittgenstein in the
Tractatus.[1] Frege indeed so far reacted against 'theories of
truth' as to declare truth to be indefinable. Now to deny that
any non-trivial *general* characterisation of the condition for a
proposition to be true is possible when the meanings of
sentences − the propositions they express − are taken as
already given is not to say that the truth-conditions of the
sentences of a particular language cannot be specified
piecemeal, or, more accurately, inductively by means of a
semantic theory for the language. Of course they can: for that
was precisely the form which Frege conceived a theory of
reference − the basis of a theory of sense − as taking. Such a
specification remains as possible as it was before: to deny the
possibility of a *general* characterisation of the truth-condition
of a *proposition* has no bearing on the possibility of a theory
yielding a *case-by-case* specification of the truth-condition of
each *sentence*. The question is not whether such an inductive
specification of truth-conditions is possible, but, rather, what
it achieves. Tarski proposed it as a *definition* of truth − that is,
of the predicate "is true" as applied to the sentences of the
given language.[2] But, if we do not yet know at all what truth
is, and if we also do not know the meanings of any expressions
of the language, such a definition will not convey the
significance of calling a sentence of that language "true".
Given an understanding of the language, the definition would
be a cumbrous means of determining that significance: so it
may be said that a Tarskian truth-definition fixes the sense of
the word "true", as applied to the sentences of a single
language, given their meanings.

   Davidson proposed to use the specification of truth-
conditions for the opposite purpose: taking the notion of truth

[1] L. Wittgenstein, *Tractatus Logico-Philosophicus*, 4.022ff.
[2] Alfred Tarski, 'Der Wahrheitsbegriff in den formalisierten Sprachen',
Studia philosophica, Vol. 1, 1935, pp. 261-405; Eng. trans. by J.H. Woodger

as already understood, to treat the theory determining the truth-conditions of sentences of the language as explaining their meanings and those of the words composing them.[3] In making this proposal, he was reverting to an approach very similar to Frege's. The differences were twofold. First, although Davidson did not need to repudiate Frege's distinction between sense and reference, he did not envisage any specification of the senses of expressions: his proposed theory would in effect be a theory of reference, from which the senses of expressions would be apparent, but in which they would not be stated.

A good case can be made that, in this respect, Davidson was not being unfaithful to Frege. In *Grundgesetze* the stipulations of the references of expressions of the symbolic language are taken by Frege as serving to *show* what their senses are without its being necessary, or perhaps even possible, to *state* them. The second divergence between a Davidsonian and a Fregean theory is, however, unarguable, and, from the present standpoint, more important, namely that Davidson proposed to dispense with a theory of force. In a theory of meaning of his type, it is not deemed necessary to describe, or even mention, the linguistic activities of making assertions, asking questions, making requests, giving advice, issuing commands, etc.: the theory will simply specify the truth-conditions of all sentences, and thereby determine the meanings of all expressions of the language.

It is of the utmost importance to an understanding of Davidson's conception that it presupposes a grasp of the concept of truth. Clearly, the concept cannot be thought of, in this context, as given by means of a Tarskian truth-definition. That would mean that the truth-definition would be stated once, to fix the sense of the predicate "is true", and then repeated all over again, intact save for this time being presented as a theory rather than as a definition, in order to

---

in A. Tarski, *Logic, Semantics, Metamathematics*, Oxford, 1956.

[3] Donald Davidson, 'Reply to Foster', in *Truth and Meaning*, ed. G. Evans and J. McDowell, Oxford, 1976; see p. 35. Reprinted in D. Davidson, *Inquiries into Truth and Interpretation*, Oxford, 1984.

give the meanings of the expressions of the language. Obviously, from this second statement of the specification of truth-conditions, we should learn nothing, since it would state only what was already embodied in its first enunciation, as a definition. Indeed, it is clear that, if we began without either understanding the language or knowing what "true" meant, we should from this procedure gain no knowledge of the meanings of the words of the language: more generally, if we know *no more* about the concept of truth than that it applies to sentences of the language as the truth-definition says that it does, we cannot learn from a statement of the condition for the truth of a sentence what that sentence means. It is essential to Davidson's project that one brings to the theory a prior understanding of the concept of truth: only so can one derive, from a specification of the truth-conditions of sentences, a grasp of what they mean.

What must such a prior understanding of the concept of truth comprise? It need not incorporate any knowledge of the conditions under which sentences of the language are true: that, after all, is going to be laid down by the truth-theory. What must be brought is a grasp of the conceptual connection between meaning and truth. That is to say, one must know, at least implicitly, how the meaning of a sentence is determined by its truth-condition. And here a grasp of the meaning of the sentence must embody an understanding of how it is to be used in linguistic interchange. Davidson himself is explicit about this: a theory of meaning for a language is to be a theory such that whoever knows it is thereby enabled to speak the language. He does not merely view its sentences as expressing thoughts – where a thought is not yet a judgement, but only the content of one: he grasps the significance of an utterance of each sentence, and can therefore respond appropriately to such an utterance, and can himself utter those sentences on appropriate occasions.

Very much has therefore been left implicit that a theory of meaning ought to make explicit. What is left implicit is that which anyone must grasp, concerning the concept of truth, in order to be able to use a Davidsonian truth-theory *as* a theory of meaning: that is in order to be able to derive, from the specification of truth-conditions, a knowledge of how to use the sentences. What he must grasp is the connection between truth and meaning: until it has been rendered explicit just what this connection is, the description of the truth-theory does not yet amount to an adequate philosophical elucidation of the concept of meaning.

And now we may say that Davidson makes the opposite mistake to that made by the proponents of the correspondence and coherence theories of truth. Their error lay in trying to give an explanation of truth, assuming meaning as already given, whereas the two concepts have to be explained *together*. But Davidson's mistake is the converse one, to try to explain meaning, assuming the concept of truth as already understood: for an adequate explanation of either, they still have to be explained *together*.

Or, at least, they have to be explained together so long as Frege's insight continues to be respected, namely that the concept of truth plays a central role in the explanation of sense. On this Fregean view, the concept of truth occupies the mid-point on the line of connection between sense and use. On the one side, the truth-condition of the sentence determines the thought it expresses, in accordance with the theory developed by Frege and adapted by Davidson; on the other, it governs the use to be made of the sentence in converse with other speakers, in accordance with the principles left tacit by both of them. That leaves open the possibility of describing the use directly, and regarding it as determining meaning, relegating the concept of truth to a minor, non-functional role. This was the course adopted by Wittgenstein in his later work. The concept of truth, no longer required to play a part in a theory explaining what it is for sentences to mean what they do, now really can be characterised on the assumption that their meanings are already given.

This is done as follows. If Brazilians speak Portuguese, and Smith says, "Brazilians speak Portuguese", then what Smith says is true. This illustrates a general principle of equivalence between a sentence containing the word "true" and another which does not: according to the present account, this equivalence principle embodies the sole point of having the word "true" in the language. The principle is precisely analogous to an explanation of the term "denote" by the general principle illustrated by saying that "Germany" denotes Germany. We need to be extremely careful with the claim that the *whole* meaning of "denote" is contained in this principle. If someone had never met the verb "denote" we might well explain it to him by saying that "Paris" denotes Paris, "Germany" denotes Germany, and so on; but if he were to respond, "And I suppose that the French word 'Allemagne' and the German word 'Deutschland' also denote Germany", he would have derived more from our explanation than just the schema " 'X' denotes X". The same holds good for the equivalence principle for "true": the schema " 'P' is true if and only if P" tells us nothing about what it is for a sentence of a language other than English to be true.

In any case, the purpose of an explanation of the concept of truth along these lines is to deny the concept any theoretical role in elucidating that of linguistic meaning. Rather than characterising meaning in terms of truth-conditions, and then explaining how the use of a sentence depends upon its meaning as so characterised, this approach requires us to give a direct description of its use: this will then *constitute* its meaning.

The disadvantage of this approach lies in its unsystematic nature. This, for Wittgenstein, was a merit: he stressed the diversity of linguistic acts and of the contributions made to sentences by words of different kinds. Systematisation is not, however, motivated solely by a passion for order: like the axiomatic presentation of a mathematical theory, it serves to isolate initial assumptions. A description of the use of a particular expression or type of sentence is likely to presuppose an understanding of a considerable part of the rest of the language: only a systematic theory can reveal how far linguistic meaning can be explained without a prior supply of semantic notions. The ideal would be to explain it without taking any such notions as given: for it would otherwise be hard to account for our coming by such notions, or to state in any non-circular manner what it is to possess them. It is unclear from Frege's work whether this ideal is attainable. The indefinability of truth does not, of itself, imply the inexplicability of truth, although Frege himself offered no satisfactory account of elucidations that fall short of being definitions. Perhaps the concept of truth can be adequately explained if a substantive analysis of the concepts of assertion and of judgement is feasible: but Frege leaves us in the dark about this. Wittgenstein, equally, leaves us in the dark about whether his programme can be executed: it is another disadvantage for the repudiation of system that it leaves us with no way of judging, in advance of the attainment of complete success, whether a strategy is likely to be successful.

CHAPTER 4

The Extrusion of Thoughts from the Mind

Such, then, was Frege's legacy to analytical philosophy: the thread ends in a knot that has yet to be unravelled. Particular features of Frege's theories contained some of the seeds of future developments: but, despite the example of *Grundlagen*, the linguistic turn, as the methodological strategy of an entire philosophical school, may still appear surprising. It was not so much the details of Frege's philosophy, filtered through the writings of a few more directly influential figures such as Russell, Wittgenstein and Carnap, that led to the linguistic turn, as a fundamental conception which he shared with other philosophical writers who used the German language.

This was the extrusion of thoughts from the mind. For Frege, thoughts – the contents of acts of thinking – are not constituents of the stream of consciousness: he asserts repeatedly that they are not contents of the mind or of consciousness as are sensations, mental images and the like – all that he includes under the general term "idea" (*Vorstellung*). He allows that grasping a thought is a mental act: but it is an act whereby the mind apprehends that which is external to it in the sense of existing independently of being grasped by that or any other subject. The reason is that thoughts are objective, whereas ideas are not. I can tell you something of what my idea is like, but it remains intrinsically *my* idea, and, for that reason, there is no telling how far it is the same as your idea. By contrast, I can communicate to you the very thought which I am entertaining or which I judge to

22

be true or false: if it were not so, we should never know whether or not we were really disagreeing. No thought, therefore, can be mine in the sense in which a sensation is mine: it is common to all, as being accessible to all. Frege maintained a very stark dichotomy between the objective and the subjective, recognising no intermediate category of the intersubjective. The subjective was for him essentially private and incommunicable; he therefore held that the existence of whatever is common to all must be independent of any. On Frege's view, thoughts and their constituent senses form a 'third realm' of timeless and immutable entities which do not depend for their existence on being grasped or expressed.[1]

The practical consequence of this ontological doctrine was the rejection of psychologism. If thoughts are not mental contents, then they are not to be analysed in terms of individual mental operations. Logic and theories of thought and of meaning are thus to be sharply demarcated from psychology. Although Frege arrived at this position quite independently, he was far from unique in holding it. Bolzano had drawn a distinction between the subjective and the objective in almost the same terms as Frege, and had anticipated his complaint that Kant fails to maintain a clear distinction between them. He had made the same distinction as Frege between subjective and objective ideas, or ideas possessed and ideas in themselves:[2] this is precisely Frege's distinction between ideas and senses. He had likewise distinguished between propositions as being thought and propositions in themselves, crediting Leibniz and Herbart with having previously made a parallel distinction. Bolzano's propositions in themselves are, of course, the equivalent of Frege's thoughts. He held, like Frege, that ideas and propositions in themselves are objective and do not depend upon our apprehension of them; but, precisely like Frege, he viewed them as not being 'actual', which he also expressed, as

---

[1] Cf. G. Frege, 'Der Gedanke', pp. 69-77; *Collected Papers*, pp. 363-72.
[2] Bernard Bolzano, *Wissenschaftslehre*, Vol. 1, 1837, §§48ff.; see B. Bolzano, *Theory of Science*, abridged Eng. trans. by J. Berg, Dordrecht, 1973.

Frege did not, by denying 'existence' to them. By this he seems
to have meant what Frege meant by speaking of thoughts and
other objects as objective but not actual, namely that they do
not enter into any causal transactions.[3] There is no reason to
suppose that Frege ever read Bolzano, but Husserl and
Meinong did, and both followed him in thus extruding
thoughts, in Frege's sense of the term, from the mind; in
Husserl's case, this happened after his initial excursion, in his
Philosophie der Arithmetik of 1891,[4] into psychologism, from
which he then recoiled to become its most vehement opponent.

Recent writers in the analytical tradition have criticised
Frege for his strongly subjective interpretation of sensations
and mental images. This criticism stems from Wittgenstein's
critique of the private ostensive definition. The critique is
aimed at the possibility of a private language, but Wittgenstein
is not concerned merely to make a point in the philosophy of
language: the argument seeks to destroy the conception of the
private object that I, but only I, can recognise. To recognise an
object when it occurs again is to make a judgement of a particular kind, and such a judgement involves what Frege calls a
thought. Wittgenstein is in effect assuming that we cannot suppose an object to exist unless it is possible to have thoughts
about it, and, in particular, to recognise it as the same again. He
is not assuming that all thoughts are expressed in language,
but he is assuming that all are expressible in language: if there
are private objects, there must be private thoughts about them,
and, if there are private thoughts, then there could be a private
language in which they were expressed. This is not to deny that
sensations are in some sense private and subjective, but it is to
deny their *radical* subjectivity after Frege's model: they are
neither incommunicable nor accessible to the subject independently of criteria available to others.

The arguments Frege puts forward to show, in opposition to
psychologism, that thoughts are not contents of the mind, are
always made by him to turn on the contrast between the

[3] G. Frege, *Grundgesetze*, Vol. I, p. xviii; 'Der Gedanke', p. 76.
[4] Edmund Husserl, *Philosophie der Arithmetik*, Halle, 1891; reprinted in
Husserliana, Vol. XII, ed. L. Eley, the Hague, 1970.

subjective and incommunicable character of "ideas" and the objective and communicable character of thoughts. It is therefore natural to think that the distinction must collapse once this subjectivist interpretation of "ideas" is abandoned. But this is a mistake; for Wittgenstein himself draws the boundary around the contents of the mind in precisely the same place as does Frege. Frege conceded that grasping a thought is a mental act, even though the thought grasped is not a content of the mind. Wittgenstein goes further by denying that understanding is a mental process; and, in doing so, he cites as genuine mental processes exactly what Frege would have classified as such: "a pain's growing more and less; the hearing of a tune or a sentence".[5]

The importance of the denial of the mental character of thoughts, common to Bolzano, Frege, Meinong and Husserl, did not lie in the philosophical mythology to which it gave rise – Frege's myth of the 'third realm', or Husserl's of 'ideal being'. It lay, rather, in the non-psychological direction given to the analysis of concepts and of propositions. It is, however, very clear why it was to lead to analytical philosophy, to the analysis of thought by means of the analysis of language. For if one accepts the initial step – the extrusion of thoughts and their components from the mind – one may yet feel unhappy with the ontological mythology which, as we have seen, was already in some tension with Frege's more detailed accounts of particular senses. One in this position has therefore to look about him to find something non-mythological but objective and external to the individual mind to embody the thoughts which the individual subject grasps and may assent to or reject. Where better to find it than in the institution of a common language? The accessibility of thoughts will then reside in their capacity for linguistic expression, and their objectivity and independence from inner mental processes in the *common* practice of speaking the language, governed by agreement among the linguistic community on standards of correct use and on criteria for the truth of statements. Given

---

[5] L. Wittgenstein, *Philosophical Investigations*, Oxford, 1953, I-154; see also p. 59, below the line.

the initial step taken by Bolzano, and followed by Frege, Meinong and Husserl, whereby thoughts were removed from the inner world of mental experience, the second step, of regarding them, not as merely transmitted, but as generated, by language, was virtually inevitable: it is puzzling only why it took so long.

Frege was the grandfather of analytical philosophy, Husserl the founder of the phenomenological school, two radically different philosophical movements. In 1903, say, how would they have appeared to any German student of philosophy who knew the work of both? Not, certainly, as two deeply opposed thinkers: rather as remarkably close in orientation, despite some divergence of interests. They may be compared with the Rhine and the Danube, which rise quite close to one another and for a time pursue roughly parallel courses, only to diverge in utterly different directions and flow into different seas. Why, then, did this happen? What small ingredient in the thought of each was eventually magnified into so great an effect?

The answer is doubtless very complex. I cannot hope to arrive at a comprehensive, or even a satisfactory, answer here. A complete answer would be of the greatest interest: it would uncover the most important, and the most perplexing, feature of the evolution of Western philosophical thought in the twentieth century, and would go far to enable both analytic philosophy and the phenomenological school to understand their own history and one another. But one likely component of the answer can here be ventured. If the linguistic turn is accepted as providing the defining characteristic of analytic philosophy, then what made it possible for the analytic school to take it, and impossible for the phenomenological school to do so, must play a major role in explaining their divergence. In order to arrive at the conception of noema, which he developed after the *Logische Untersuchungen*, from 1907 on, Husserl *generalised* the notion of sense or meaning. Something like sense, but more general, must inform every mental act; not merely those involving linguistic expression or capable of linguistic expression, but acts of sensory perception, for example. An initial favourable response is natural: surely at least a vague analogy is possible between the particular way something is given to us when we understand an expression referring to it and the particular way an object is given to us when we perceive it by means of one of our sense-organs. And yet the generalisation precludes the linguistic turn: language can play no especial part in the study and description of these non-linguistic animators of non-linguistic mental acts. Frege's notion of sense, by contrast, was incapable of generalisation. Senses, for him, even if not intrinsically the senses of linguistic expressions, were intrinsically apt to be expressed in language; they stood in the closest connection with the truth of thoughts of which they were constituents. Hence nothing that was not a sense could be in the least *like* a sense; and so philosophers who were faithful to Frege's fundamental ideas were able to take the linguistic turn, and, as previously explained, had strong incentive for doing so. Since perception is that mental act least obviously fitted to be expressed in words, we must in due course scrutinise the views of the two innovators concerning it.

CHAPTER 5

The Legacy of Brentano

Franz Brentano's most celebrated contribution to philosophy was his introduction, or re-introduction, of the concept of intentionality, although he himself never used precisely that term. By introducing it, Brentano bequeathed a problem to his successors, one that was to be the subject of intense discussion by them: the problem of 'objectless presentations' (*gegenstandslose Vorstellungen*). The problem will best be known to British readers from Russell, whose theory of descriptions constituted his solution of it. It is difficult to say that Brentano himself discussed the problem; in his writings, what promise to be discussions of it always slide off into some other topic, leaving what seems to us the central problem unresolved.

Famously, Brentano treated intentionality as the defining characteristic of what he called mental phenomena, distinguishing them from the phenomena he termed 'physical'. It is important that the contrast he drew was between mental and physical *phenomena*, not between mental and physical *acts*. The phenomena he classified as mental were all of them acts or attitudes. Explaining his use of the term "presentation" (*Vorstellung*), Brentano went on to characterise the very broad range of things he included among mental phenomena as follows:

> Hearing a sound, seeing a coloured object, feeling warmth or cold, as well as similar states of imagination are examples of what I mean by this term ["presentation"]. I also mean by it the

28

thinking of a general concept, provided that such a thing actually does occur. Furthermore, every judgement, every recollection, every expectation, every inference, every conviction or opinion, every doubt, is a mental phenomenon. Also to be included under this term is every emotion: joy, sorrow, fear, hope, courage, despair, anger, love, hate, desire, act of will, intention, astonishment, admiration, contempt, etc.[1]

Thus presentations are considered as a species of mental phenomenon. For Brentano, it is in fact the primary species, in that all mental acts that are not themselves presentations involve presentations, and it is the presentation that gives any such act its intentional character.[2]

The intentional character of a mental act consists in its being directed towards an object. No one can simply be afraid, simply admire or simply be astonished: if anyone is afraid, he must be afraid *of* something, if he feels admiration, he must admire something or somebody, and, if he is astonished, he must be astonished *at* something. In the most often quoted passage in his writings, Brentano expressed it as follows:

> Every mental phenomenon is characterised by what the mediaeval Scholastics called the intentional (or simply mental) inexistence of an object [*Gegenstand*], and what we might call, though not quite unambiguously, reference to a content, direction towards an object [*Objekt*] (by which is not to be understood here something of the character of a thing [*eine Realität*]), or immanent objectuality. Every mental phenomenon includes something as object [*Objekt*] in itself, although they do not all do so in the same way. In a presentation something is presented, in a judgement something is affirmed or denied, in love something is loved, in hate something is

---

[1] F. Brentano, *Psychologie vom empirischen Standpunkt*, Leipzig, 1874, Book II, chap. 1, section 2, p. 108: English translation by Linda L. McAlister, *Psychology from an Empirical Standpoint*, London, 1973, p. 79.
[2] *Psychologie*, Book II, chap. 1, section 3, p. 104 and chap. 9, section 2, p. 348; *Psychology*, pp. 80 and 266-7.

hated, in desire something is desired, and so forth.[3]

The physical phenomena which Brentano contrasts with mental ones, as lacking the characteristic of intentionality, were not transactions in the physical world, as we understand it, but were still *phenomena*. Brentano took them to be phenomenal qualities, such as colours and auditory tones, and complexes of them; as he says:

> Examples of physical phenomena ... are: a colour, a shape, a panorama which I see; a chord which I hear; warmth, cold, an odour which I experience; and also similar images which appear in the imagination.[4]

Brentano insists that the 'physical phenomena' thus circumscribed never exhibit anything like the characteristic of 'intentional inexistence'. The point insisted on needs no argument. His 'physical phenomena' are not acts in even the most general sense, and therefore cannot be referred to by means of transitive verbs; it would thus be literally ungrammatical to speak of them as having, or, equally, as lacking, objects. Brentano concludes that we may "define mental phenomena by saying that they are those phenomena which contain an object intentionally within themselves".[5] What he meant by "contain an object intentionally within themselves" can best be understood by drawing a contrast he does not draw, between a mental act in his sense and what we should ordinarily call a physical act, for instance that of kicking a football. The object of such an act is extrinsic to it *qua* physical act. Up to the point of contact, the act of kicking the football would have been exactly the same if the ball had

[3] *Psychologie*, Book II, chap. 1, section 5, p. 115; *Psychology*, p. 88. German has two words, *Gegenstand* and *Objekt*, where English has only one, "object". With these primary words, nothing can be done to distinguish them in translation save to put the German word in brackets; but I have sought to distinguish *objektiv/Objektivität* from *gegenständlich/Gegenständlichkeit* by translating the former "objective, -ity" and the latter "objectual, -ity".

[4] *Psychologie*, Book II, chap. 1, section 2, p. 104; *Psychology*, pp. 79-80.

[5] *Psychologie*, Book II, chap. 1, section 5, p. 116; *Psychology*, p. 89.

not been there: it is only to the intention underlying the act that the object is intrinsic, in that I should not have had precisely the same intention if I had meant merely to make a kicking motion without impact. In a different terminology, the relation of such a physical act to its object is external, that of a mental act to its object internal.

Brentano was not at fault in making the object intrinsic to the mental act: Wittgenstein, too, insisted that the relation between an expectation and the event expected, or between an intention and its fulfilment, is an internal, even a 'grammatical' one.[6] Brentano's words appear, however, to do more than this: to attribute to the object a special kind of existence. On such an interpretation, an object may have either or both of two modes of existence: it may exist in the actual world, external to the mind; and it may also exist in the mind, as incorporated in a mental act directed towards it. There would then be no more difficulty in explaining how there can be a mental act directed towards something that has no actual existence than in admitting the actual existence of objects to which no mental act is directed: in the former case, the object would have intentional inexistence but no existence in actuality, while in the latter it would exist in actuality while lacking any intentional inexistence. It is necessary to admit the possibility of the latter case if we are to be realists about the external world; it is necessary to admit the possibility of the former if we are to recognise that the mind is not constrained by external reality. It is but a short step from such a position to the thesis that the object of *any* mental act is to be considered as enjoying only mental inexistence, but that it *represents* the external object, if there is one. According to such a development from Brentano's view, a mental act is always directed towards something which, as an ingredient of the act, is essentially a content of the mind; at this stage, we have planted both feet in the bog of empiricism and can no longer save ourselves from being relentlessly sucked into it.

[6] See L. Wittgenstein, *Philosophical Investigations*, Oxford, 1953, I-§§445, 458, 476, etc.

But that was not the road down which Brentano travelled. It seems probable that when, in the original edition of *Psychologie vom empirischen Standpunkt* of 1874, he employed the term "intentional inexistence", he did mean to ascribe to the objects of mental acts a special kind of existence in the mind, distinguishable from actual existence. But he withdrew from the edge of the bog. He not only declined to take the next step into full-blooded representationalism: he came to repudiate the conception of a shadowy mental existence altogether. He very properly continued to maintain that the object of a mental act is intrinsic to the act; but he nevertheless now insisted that it is external to the mind, in the strong sense of "external". In the weak sense of "external", an external object merely stands opposed to an internal one, where an internal object is the correlate of a cognate accusative: the internal object of thinking, in this sense of "internal", is a thought. With this internal object we may contrast an external one, in this case that which is being thought about; but this is only the weak sense of "external". In the strong sense of the term, an external object is one that is not a constituent of the subject's consciousness, but a part of the objective world independent of him and of the mental act he directs towards it: it was as external in this strong sense that, from about 1905 onwards, Brentano came to think of the object of a mental act. If, for instance, I intend to marry a woman, or promise to marry her, it is *that woman* whom I intend or promise to marry, and who is therefore the object of my mental act, whether expressed or unexpressed: the object of that mental act is not my inner representation of the woman, but the woman herself. And that is how Brentano came to view it. "It is paradoxical in the extreme to say that a man promises to marry an *ens rationis* and fulfils his promise by marrying a real person", he wrote in 1909.[7]

[7] Letter to Oskar Kraus dated 1909 and quoted by Kraus in his Introduction to the second edition of *Psychologie*, Leipzig, 1924; see *Psychology*, p. 385. Barry Smith, in footnote 3 of his 'On the Origins of Analytic Philosophy', *Grazer philosophische Studien*, Vol. 35, 1989, pp. 153-73, maintains that the context deprives this remark of the meaning

Thus, when a mental act is directed towards something that exists in actuality, it is that very object, considered as actually existing, that is the object of the mental act. Does not this leave it open that the object has also a different type of existence, as a constituent of the mental act, and that, when the object of a mental act lacks actual existence, it has only this mental type of existence? Not according to the later Brentano: for, on his later view, there are not, properly speaking, any different *types* of existence at all: there is only actual existence, and all other ways of speaking, though frequently convenient, are, strictly speaking, improper:

> All mental references refer to things (*Dinge*). In many cases, the things to which we refer do not exist. We are, however, accustomed to say that they then have being as objects [of the mental acts]. This is an improper use of the verb "to be", which we permit ourselves for the sake of convenience, just as we speak of the Sun's "rising" or "setting". All that it means is that a mentally active subject is referring to those things.[8]

This passage contains another retractation. In the famous passage quoted above from the *Psychologie vom empirischen Standpunkt* in which Brentano formulated the thesis of intentionality, he went out of his way to assert that the object of a mental act need not be a '*Realität*'. Brentano used the word "*real*" and its cognates much like Frege's "actual" (*wirklich*), to mean 'involved in causal interactions', and the word "thing" (*Ding*) for the narrower class of concrete particulars, which, for him, might be either material or spiritual: in effect, substances in Descartes's sense. Not only did he think, at the time of the *Psychologie*, that the object of a mental act need not be a thing in this sense, but he had allowed that it might be a 'content', meaning the content of a proposition. His later view was that the object of a mental

---

which it appears on its face to bear. I have not been able to see that this is so, or to understand what other meaning it can possibly have.

[8] Supplementary Remark 9, added to F. Brentano, *Von der Klassifikation der psychischen Phänomena*, Leipzig, 1911, which was a reissue of Book 2 of the *Psychologie* with eleven Supplementary Remarks, p. 145. See *Psychology*, p. 291.

act could only be a thing (whether or not it actually existed).
In other words, all mental acts must be directed at concrete
particulars as their objects. This naturally led Brentano into
some very involved attempts to explain away a host of
apparent counter-examples. His general strategy for doing
this was to admit a large variety of different 'modes of
presentation', that is, of different types of mental act
involving different relations to their objects. In this way, he
repudiated the entire range of ideal objects admitted by
Husserl and Meinong, or of those objects characterised by
Frege as objective but not 'actual', whose existence he claimed
we must acknowledge if we are to avoid physicalism on the
one hand and psychologism on the other. About Meinong's
'objectives' – the equivalents of Frege's 'thoughts' – Brentano
was especially scathing.

How, then, can Brentano blandly state, in the passage just
quoted, that "in many cases the things to which we refer" –
that is, the objects of our mental acts – "do not exist"? As
Føllesdal rightly observes,[9] Brentano's eventual endorsement
of the view that, when the object actually exists, it is that very
object, and not any mental representation of it, which is the
object of the mental act tallies exactly with the way Frege
understood the reference of a proper name. For him, when I
speak of the Moon, it is the heavenly body itself, and not my
idea of the Moon, to which the phrase I use refers, and hence it
is *about* that heavenly body that I am talking.

> ... when we say "the Moon", we do not intend to speak of our
> idea of the Moon, nor are we satisfied with the sense alone, but
> we presuppose a reference. To assume that in the sentence
> "The Moon is smaller than the Earth" the idea of the Moon is in
> question would be flatly to misunderstand the sense. If this is
> what the speaker wanted, he would use the phrase "my idea of
> the Moon".[10]

[9] D. Føllesdal, 'Brentano and Husserl on Intentional Objects and
Perception', in H. L. Dreyfus (ed.), *Husserl, Intentionality and Cognitive
Science*, Cambridge, Mass., and London, 1982, pp. 31-41; see p. 32.
[10] G. Frege, 'Über Sinn und Bedeutung' (1892), p. 31.

But this only leaves it unexplained how there may be a genuine mental act, even though there is in fact no object: I may be frightened by or amused at something illusory, and, above all, I may be the victim of a hallucination or other sensory delusion. These still have the characteristic of intentionality: a visual or auditory illusion is not an instance of simply seeing or hearing without seeing or hearing anything. To have that characteristic is to be directed towards an object; but, by hypothesis, there is no object in such a case. We cannot say that, in *these* cases, the object is, after all, a constituent of the subject's mind; for, if we say that, we cannot resist saying the same in a case of veridical perception. As Frege pointed out, this escape-route may easily be blocked verbally; if, for instance, the subject is under the illusion that an oak-tree is before him, and makes some statement about it, then, if a hearer suggests that he is referring to his idea of an oak-tree, he may say something like, "I am not talking about any idea, but about that actual tree there". Here the subject's intention is paramount: if he declares that what he means to refer to is an oak-tree, and not the idea of one, then, although he may not in fact be referring to any oak-tree, he certainly cannot be referring to anything but an oak-tree. Similarly with unexpressed thoughts. A subject may not be thinking of anything at all: but he cannot be thinking of that which he expressly means not to be thinking of.

Brentano evidently deemed it sufficient to observe that "if someone thinks of something, the one who is thinking must certainly exist, but the object of his thinking need not exist at all".[11] This is quite obviously inadequate: for what does the phrase "the object of his thinking" stand for here? Meinong solved the problem by denying that there are or could be any 'objectless presentations'; it was only our prejudice in favour of the actual that led us to think there were. Not all objects exist; only some of them do, and our referring to or thinking about those that do not is no more problematic than our referring to or thinking about those that do. Such a solution

[11] *Klassifikation*, Supplementary Remark 1, p. 123; *Psychology*, p. 272.

was not available to Brentano, who vehemently denied the admissibility of any notion of 'being' distinct from 'existence'. If, on the other hand, it were denied that "the object of his thinking" stands for anything at all, that would be to equate the statement "The object of his thinking does not exist" with "His thinking does not have an object"; and that would flatly contradict Brentano's fundamental principle that every mental act is directed towards an object, and hence, in particular, that one is thinking must be thinking of something, a thesis difficult to construe otherwise than as meaning that there is something of which he is thinking. It was not open to Brentano, either, to say that in *such* a case, the object of the mental act is after all a constituent of the subject's mind, but not in a case when the object does exist: such a position would be unstable, and quickly collapse into the view that the object of a mental act resides within the subject's consciousness in *every* case. Intentionality is naturally taken to be a relation between the mental act, or its subject, to the object of the act: but how can there be a relation when the second term of the relation does not exist?

This was, then, the problem Brentano bequeathed to his successors. Frege, during his early period, that is to say, up to 1890, drew no distinction between signification and thing signified; he used the term "content" indifferently for both. He therefore drew the consequence that when an empty singular term occurred in a sentence, that sentence was devoid of content: if a part lacks content, the whole must lack content, too.[12] From 1891 onwards, however, he distinguished sense and reference within his former undifferentiated notion of content; henceforward he had this distinction by means of which to explain the matter. An empty name, though it lacks a reference, may still possess a sense. A sentence containing it

---

[12] "The sentence 'Leo Sachse is a man' is the expression of a thought only if 'Leo Sachse' designates something. And so too the sentence 'This table is round' is the expression of a thought only if the words 'this table' are not empty sounds but designate something specific for me." From an early set of remarks on Lotze's *Logik*: see G. Frege, *Posthumous Writings*, ed. P. Long and R. White, Oxford, 1979, p. 174.

cannot be true or false, since, if a part lacks reference, the whole must lack reference, and the reference of a sentence, on Frege's theory, is a truth-value; but the sentence will still express a thought if the name has a sense. There is thus no simple answer to the question whether a speaker who uttered such a sentence would thereby have *said* anything: he expressed a thought, but he said nothing either true or false.

There remains some awkwardness even in this mature Fregean theory; but its author rested content with it. Unlike Husserl and Meinong, he was not a follower of Brentano, and hence was not committed to the thesis of intentionality, to the effect that every mental act has an object: he therefore had no need to be at pains to reconcile his theory with that thesis. What is remarkable is that Husserl arrived, only a short time later, at essentially the same conclusion.

In an unpublished essay, 'Intentionale Gegenstände', which Husserl wrote in 1894, he concluded that the 'objectual intention' is *not* a relation, but a property of the objective content of the mental act.[13] This property is what we call 'presenting an object' or 'referring to (*Meinen*) an object'. The content of the act is to be identified with a meaning (*Bedeutung*), conceived of as strictly parallel with the meanings expressed in linguistic utterances. "The meaning alone is the intrinsic and essential characteristic of a presentation [*Vorstellung*], whereas the objectual reference indicates certain connections of truths and of judgements into which that meaning enters."[14] That is to say, actual or hypothetical reference to an object is a feature of the meaning explicable in terms of its role in inferential relations.

The convergence of view between Frege and Husserl at this stage is striking. As Husserl developed his ideas in the

[13] Published in *Husserliana*, Vol. XXII, ed. B. Rang, the Hague, 1979; the first part, having been lost, was omitted. Now further parts of the text have been found, and a new edition published in *Brentano-Studien*, Vol. 3, 1990-1, pp. 137-76, with commentary by Karl Schuhmann. For an illuminating discussion of this essay, see H. Philipse, 'The Concept of Intentionality: Husserl's Development from the Brentano Period to the *Logical Investigations*', *Philosophy Research Archives*, Vol. XII, 1987, pp. 293-328, section VI.

[14] *Husserliana*, Vol. XXII, p. 336; see H. Philipse, op. cit., p. 312.

Logische Untersuchungen of 1900-1, the affinity became yet closer. Husserl distinguished between the *matter* and the *quality* of any mental act, holding that acts that differed in quality might have their matter in common.[15] The quality here corresponds to what Frege called the 'force' attached to an utterance, which distinguishes an assertion from a question whose content (sense) may be the same; the difference is that Husserl does not share Frege's caution, but is prepared to admit a great variety of distinct qualities. The 'matter' corresponds to Frege's sense: Husserl explains that he refrains from using the word "meaning" for this purpose because the quality might be thought to be part of the meaning; he is of course quite right that we should regard an assertoric sentence and the corresponding interrogative as differing in meaning. He is clear that a difference in the object referred to must imply a difference in the matter, but that there may be a difference between the matter of two acts, although they both refer to the same object. This exactly parallels Frege's view that a difference in reference entails a difference in sense, but that the senses of two expressions may differ though the reference remains constant.

Furthermore, from the time of *Logische Untersuchungen* onwards, Husserl distinguished sharply between objective meanings and subjective ideas, as Frege had already done in his *Grundlagen* of 1884 and as Bolzano had done before him. Making such a distinction was an integral part of Husserl's revulsion from the psychologism he had originally espoused, but of which, in alliance with Frege, he now became the leading opponent.

There are notable differences between them, all the same. Frege applied his theories all but exclusively to thoughts and the sentences that express them. He was concerned, therefore, only with those mental acts or attitudes that can be conveyed by means of language: what Russell called 'propositional attitudes', in other words, those that can be ascribed to another by means of a sentence involving a "that"-clause (*oratio obliqua*).

---

[15] *Logische Untersuchingen*, Halle, 1900-1, 1913, Investigation V, §20.

Husserl's 'meaning' corresponds to Frege's 'sense'; but he boldly applies it, not only to what he called 'expressive' acts, carried out by means of linguistic utterance, but to all mental acts without qualification, that is, all that exhibit the phenomenon of intentionality. Plainly, meaning, for him, was independent of language, even if apt to be expressed in words. Senses were independent of language for Frege, too, in that their existence did not depend upon their being expressed; but he held, at the same time, that *we* can grasp them only through their verbal or symbolic expression. It certainly appears that Husserl was here engaged in an ambitious generalisation.

Furthermore, Husserl's conception of reference remained distressingly vague. Frege's notion of reference (*Bedeutung* in *his* somewhat eccentric sense) was unwaveringly directed at the determination of truth-value: to assign a reference to an expression was to declare its role in the mechanism whereby any sentence in which it occurred was determined as true or as false. He therefore had a clear principle for deciding what the reference of expressions of any logical category should be taken to be. Husserl lacked such a principle, and, lacking it, was hazy about what expressions other than singular terms should be taken to refer to: he makes a convincing case for a distinction between meaning and objectual correlate only for singular terms. In particular, he thought of a predicate or general term as referring to the individual objects to which it applied, whereas Frege held the reference of such a predicate to be a concept. For Frege, the fact that there were no objects to which a predicate applied (no objects falling under the concept) did not signify that it was devoid of reference, and hence did not threaten a sentence containing it with deprivation of truth-value; on Husserl's view, the class of mental acts, including expressive acts, lacking objectual correlates would of necessity be much wider.

There is a persistent philosophical tendency, which, among analytic philosophers, has been somewhat in the ascendant lately, to repudiate any notion of sense in favour of that of reference alone. Russell of course exemplified this tendency, presumably because he feared that to admit the notion of sense would threaten his realism. The tendency is particularly strong when singular terms are under consideration. The thesis of 'direct reference', namely that the sole linguistic feature of a proper name, strictly so called, consists in its reference, is undoubtedly attractive at first glance; it would be absurd if applied to complex terms such as definite descriptions. Those inclined to accept this thesis are therefore bound to maintain that definite descriptions are not genuine singular terms; the ground for this contention now popular is their behaviour, different from that of proper names, in modal and temporal contexts. As Gareth Evans observed, however, even if the contention be allowed, there are proper names whose reference is fixed descriptively: the attribution to them of meanings or senses is as compelling as to definite descriptions, while the ground is lacking to deny them the title of singular terms.[16]

The tendency, which is perennial, is also retrograde; but Husserl was unaffected by it. He saw nothing problematic in ascribing meanings to singular terms, and distinguishing them from the objects they denote, just as Frege distinguished between their senses and their references. It is quite unnecessary to attribute Husserl's making this distinction to Frege's influence, as some have done: granted a willingness to ascribe a meaning or sense to a singular term, it lies to hand to distinguish between it and the reference of the term. We come to the analysis of how language functions already armed with the notion of referring to something by means of a singular term, the notion, that is, of using the term to talk about a particular object: no one ever had to *argue* that singular terms, in general, have reference. The only problematic question, therefore, is whether it is right to attribute to such a term a sense distinct from its having the reference it has. The sense or meaning of a singular term, including a proper name, is the way the object it refers to is given to someone in virtue of his knowing the language to which the term belongs: otherwise expressed, it is the means

[16] G. Evans, *The Varieties of Reference*, ed. J. McDowell, Oxford, 1982, pp. 46-51.

he has for knowing what kind of object it refers to, and picking out the particular such object it denotes. So expressed, it can hardly be doubted that, for any one individual speaker, there must be some such sense he attaches to the term, tracing a particular path to the relevant object. It needs further argument to establish that any particular such sense is a characteristic of the language, that must be known to a speaker if he is to understand sentences containing it as they are intended. Such an argument will turn on what is demanded for communication: if two speakers are to communicate successfully, they have not only to use a given name or other term as referring to the same object, but must be able to *know* that they are doing so, which they can do only if they attach the same sense to it. It is on the basis of such considerations that it can be concluded that singular terms possess senses that amount to more than their having the reference that they have, senses which may differ even though the reference is the same. With ingenuity, those influenced by the thesis of direct reference may devise clever ways of countering these arguments; it is therefore the attribution of senses to singular terms, and not the attribution to them of reference, that is controversial. Husserl had no sympathy with the thesis of direct reference; he therefore could not but draw a distinction between the meaning and the object in full analogy with Frege's distinction between the sense and the reference.

Matters stand quite differently with complete sentences and with subsentential expressions other than singular terms. Here the problem is reversed: it is uncontroversial that they have meanings, whereas our instinctive reaction is to recoil from the attribution to them of reference: it is everyone's *first* reaction on reading Frege that his extension of his notion of reference from singular terms to sentences, predicates and all other significant expressions is unwarranted. What needs arguing in this case, therefore, is that these expressions are properly credited with a reference as well as with a sense of meaning. Husserl was not troubled on this score, either; he concurred with Frege in regarding all

meaningful expressions as having, or at least purporting to
have, objectual reference (*gegenständliche Beziehung*). That,
indeed, is the point of his using the word "objectuality"
(*Gegenständlichkeit*): he explained his employment of it on
the ground that reference is not always to an *object* properly
so called. As much as Frege did, though not on the same
ground that every significant expression in a sentence has a
role in the determination of its truth-value, Husserl took it for
granted that meaningful expressions of all types, and not just
singular terms, have reference; and that is another aspect of
the remarkable agreement between them at the beginning of
the century.

CHAPTER 6

Husserl's View of Meaning

It was due to his inheritance from Brentano that Husserl took for granted that, in general, meaningful expressions have reference. For a follower of Brentano, all mental acts are characterised by intentionality, and therefore have, or at least purport to have, objects. An utterance is not, of course, in itself a mental act: but its having the significance it does is due, on Husserl's account, to its being informed by a certain mental act – what he called the meaning-conferring act. For him, indeed, this meaning-conferring act was not a *separate* mental act lying behind the physical act of utterance and investing it with significance – the conception against which Wittgenstein inveighed.[1] Rather, there is just a *single* act, that of uttering the words *as* having certain meanings, which has two aspects or constituents, one physical and the other mental.

> If we assume a stance of pure description, the concrete phenomenon of the expression given life by its sense splits into the *physical phenomenon*, on the one hand, in which the expression constitutes itself in its physical aspect, and, on the other, into the *acts* which give it *meaning*, and possibly also intuitive fulfilment, and in which the reference to an

---

[1] L. Wittgenstein, *Philosophical Investigations*, Oxford, 1953: "When I think in language, there aren't 'meanings' going through my mind in addition to the linguistic expression; but the language is itself the vehicle of the thinking" (I-329); "Thinking is not an incorporeal process which lends life and sense to speaking, and which one could detach from speech" (I-339).

expressed objectuality is constituted.[2]

It is clear that Husserl's view that there is only a single composite act is to be preferred to the view attacked by Wittgenstein, that the physical act of uttering a sentence is *accompanied* by an interior act of attaching a meaning to it. It does not follow that Husserl had the very same view of the matter as Wittgenstein. For Wittgenstein, what confers on the speaker's words the meanings that they have is not a mental constituent of a composite act that he performs, but the *context*, which includes his knowing the language to which his sentence belongs: he *does* nothing but utter the words.[3] For Husserl, by contrast, something *occurs* in the speaker's mind: a mental act, although not an independent act, but one that is an integral part of a composite act, part physical and part mental.

The Husserl of the *Logische Untersuchungen* of course concurred with Frege in denying that senses or meanings are created by us or owe their existence to being grasped by us; but, as we have already noted in connection with Frege, this leaves it unexplained how a particular sense is attached to a particular expression. It is difficult to acquit Husserl of maintaining a view of the matter like Humpty Dumpty's:[4] the view, namely, that an utterance assumes the meaning that it bears in virtue of an interior act of investing it with that meaning. Consider, for instance, a passage from the *Formale und Transzendentale Logik* of 1929:

[2] E. Husserl, *Logische Untersuchungen*, Halle, 1900-1, second revised edn. 1913, reprinted Tübingen, 1980; trans. J. N. Findlay, *Logical Investigations*, London, 1970: Investigation I, §9.

[3] *Philosophical Investigations*, I-584: "Suppose, now, that I sit in my room and hope that N.N. will come and bring me some money; and suppose one minute of this state of affairs could be cut out of its context in isolation: would what happened during it then not be hope? – Think, for example, of the words which you may utter during this time. They no longer belong to this language. And in other circumstances the institution of money does not exist, either."

[4] Lewis Carroll, *Through the Looking-Glass*, London, 1887: " 'When *I* use a word', Humpty Dumpty said in a rather scornful tone, 'it means just what I choose it to mean – neither more nor less' " (Chapter VI).

In speaking we are continuously performing an internal act of meaning which fuses with the words and, as it were, gives them life. The effect of thus giving them life is that the words and the entire utterance as it were *embody* in themselves a meaning, and bear it embodied in them as their sense.[5]

Of late, linguists have inclined to give more credit to Humpty Dumpty than to Alice, deriding her for thinking that words have meanings independently of any particular person's meaning something by them;[6] philosophers, on the other hand, are likely to find it preposterous to ascribe Humpty Dumpty's view to a serious philosopher such as Husserl. One might, however, seek to defend the view so ascribed by reference to the employment of an ambiguous word: the speaker may use the word, either oblivious to the alternative sense he does not intend, although he knows it perfectly well, or vividly conscious of the ambiguity, but confident that his hearers will understand the word as he means it. Yet such a defence would not succeed: in neither case does the speaker's intending the word to be taken in a particular sense consist in his performing an inner act of imbuing it with that sense.[7]

What is the essence of Humpty Dumpty's view? Contrary to Husserl's idea that the meaning-intention and the utterance fuse as inseparable components or 'moments' of a single act,

[5] E. Husserl, 'Formale und Transzendentale Logik', *Jahrbuch für Philosophie und phänomenologische Forschung*, Vol. 10, 1929 (pp. 1-298), §3, p. 20; reprinted as *Formale und Transzendentale Logik* in *Husserliana*, Vol. XVII, ed. P. Janssen, the Hague, 1974, pp. 26-7; English trans. by D. Cairns, *Formal and Transcendental Logic*, the Hague, 1969, p. 22.

[6] " 'But "glory" doesn't mean "a nice knock-down argument" ' ", Alice objected": *Through the Looking-Glass*, Chapter VI.

[7] "If I say 'Mr. Scot is not a Scot', I mean the first 'Scot' as a proper name, the second one as a common name. Then do different things have to go on in my mind at the first and second 'Scot'? (Assuming that I am not uttering the sentence 'parrot-fashion'.) – Try to mean the first 'Scot' as a common name and the second one as a proper name. – How is it done? When *I* do it, I blink with the effort as I try to parade the right meanings before my mind in saying the words. – But do I parade the meanings of the words before my mind when I make the ordinary use of them?": Wittgenstein, *Philosophical Investigations*, II-ii (p. 176).

Humpty Dumpty doubtless thought of his meaning 'a nice knock-down argument' as separable from his uttering the word "glory". His doing so, however, is inessential: what matters is his belief that it is the speaker's mental act on the occasion of the utterance that confers on it its meaning. Davidson attempts to refute this on the ground that "he cannot mean what he says he means" by "There's glory for you" because he knows that Alice cannot interpret it as meaning that; when Alice says, "I don't know what you mean by 'glory' ", he shows that he knows that by replying, "Of course you don't – till I tell you."[8] This indeed captures one sense of "mean", namely 'intend to convey': you cannot intend to convey something by your words unless you expect, or at least hope, that your hearer will understand them as meaning that. But in the phrase "understand (or: take) the words to mean ...", the word "mean" does not mean 'intend to convey'. As Davidson observes, Humpty Dumpty *knows* that he will not convey his meaning to Alice unless he tells her what it is; so, when he claims to mean by "glory" 'a nice knock-down argument', he is not saying that that is what he is intending to convey by the word. Obviously, if success in conveying something to someone by means of an expression consists in his taking it to mean what I meant by it, or what I intended that he should take it to mean, it takes us no further forward in explaining what meaning is – what it is to attach a given significance to an expression – to explain that, in one use of "mean", it is equivalent to "intend to convey". If, under the stress of emotion, or the shock of some unexpected occurrence, I blurt out something I had intended to keep to myself, I am not intending to convey anything, and may hope that my hearers do *not* understand. One of them may nevertheless ask another, "What did he mean by that, I wonder?" It was in *this* sense of "mean" that Humpty Dumpty asserted that by "glory" he meant 'a nice knock-down argument', and, in general, that he meant by his words just what he chose them to mean. Husserl, in writing about meaning, was not concerned with communication, but with what a speaker means, whether

[8] D. Davidson, 'A Nice Derangement of Epitaphs', in E. LePore (ed.), *Truth and Interpretation*, Oxford, 1986, p. 440.

he succeeds in conveying it or not. With this clarification of what Humpty Dumpty was maintaining, we may ask once more whether Husserl can be acquitted of adopting Humpty Dumpty's view.

Logic, according to Husserl in the *Logical Investigations*, "has to do exclusively with those *ideal* unities that we are here calling *meanings*".[9] These 'ideal meanings' have strong similarities with Frege's 'senses'. In calling them 'ideal', he meant something closely akin to Frege's contention that senses are not 'actual' (*wirklich*), namely that they are immutable and timeless, engage in no causal transactions with other objects and do not depend for their existence upon our expressing them or apprehending them. In explaining what they are, however, Husserl adopts a view quite alien to Frege's way of thinking. "Meanings constitute ... a class of *concepts* in the sense of '*universal objects*' ", he tells us.[10] The identity-relation proper to them

> is none other than the *identity of the species*. In this way, but only in this way, can it, as an ideal unity, comprise the dispersed multiplicity of individual units ... The manifold individual units for the ideally-one meaning [*zur ideal-einen Bedeutung*] are naturally the corresponding act-moments of the act of meaning [*Aktmomente des Bedeutens*], the *meaning-intentions*. The meaning [*Bedeutung*] is therefore related to the respective acts of meaning [*Akten des Bedeutens*] ... as red, as a species, is related to the slips of paper lying here, which all 'have' this same red.[11]

Thus the 'ideal meanings' are species or universals, standing to individual acts of meaning as type to token; that is what gives them their ideal character. The relation of type to tokens is quite different from that of prototype to examplars or copies. We can understand what the prototype is without so much as knowing that it *is* a prototype or has copies; but to

[9] *Logische Untersuchungen*, Investigation I, Chapter 3, §29.
[10] Ibid., Chapter 4, §31.
[11] Ibid. I apologise for the lameness of the translation; Husserl is particularly difficult to translate, and I wanted to stick as closely to his wording as possible.

grasp the concept of a type, we have first to know what any one of its tokens is, and then to understand what equivalence relation makes them tokens of that type. Grasping the equivalence relation can be in principle quite subtle. One of the best known type/token relations is that of a (type) word to a (token) utterance of that word. A child finds this extremely easy to apprehend; but it certainly is not a simple matter of similarity of sound. Different utterances of the same word may differ in volume, pitch, timbre and speed: the feature of these various sounds that makes them all utterances of the same word is that captured by its rendering in the International Phonetic Alphabet, which depends upon what the different speakers do with their mouths to produce the sounds. The child does not know this, but he can readily perceive the relevant similarity, ignoring the irrelevant differences. To know what a type word is, one must grasp that similarity. One must, of course, also know what the tokens are of which it is the type, which, in this case, is unproblematic.

Hence, to understand what Husserl's 'ideal meanings' are, we have first to understand the nature of the 'meaning-intentions', and then to grasp what relation must obtain between any two such meaning-intentions for them to be tokens of the same type and so exemplify the same ideal meaning. Husserl is, however, far more anxious to establish the general character, on his theory, of the ideal meanings, as species or universals, than to explain what precisely an individual meaning-intention is; and of the nature of the similarity relation that constitutes them as belonging to the same species we receive even less enlightenment. This is not the major ground of criticism of the theory Husserl expounds in the *Logische Untersuchungen*, however. The major objection is that, *however* meaning-intentions be explained, the meaning of an expression cannot stand to the meaning of a particular utterance of it as type to token. To treat it as such requires that the meanings of particular utterances must be taken as primary in the order of explanation, that is, as antecedent to the ideal meanings that transcend particular occasions. When we have grasped what the tokens are, we still have to have it explained what relation renders them tokens of the same type, as we have seen; but we must certainly *first* be able to identify a token of the appropriate kind. We can understand this, as applied to meanings, only as entailing that what endows the utterance, considered as a physical phenomenon – a sound – with its significance is the meaning-conferring act. Its significance cannot be explained by appeal to the ideal meaning, since its assignment to that species is, in the conceptual order, *subsequent* to its bearing that significance, in virtue of the equivalence, in the relevant respect, between it and the significance of other utterances.

This, however, is the wrong way round. It in effect presupposes Humpty Dumpty's theory, that a word, as uttered on a particular occasion, bears whatever meaning it does because the speaker invests it with that meaning. It may be added that, if a large number of people invest it with the same meaning, the fact will come to be widely known that that is what an utterance of it usually means, and that in consequence that meaning will accrue to it as a word of the common language. But, on the contrary, a word of a language does not bear the meaning that it does because a large number of people have chosen to confer that meaning upon it; they use it as having that meaning because that is the meaning it has in the language. It is of course true that a speaker may have a false impression of what a word means in the language; and he may nevertheless succeed in conveying what he intended to say, because the hearers guess what mistake he was making. Not only that, but those who did not themselves know the word, and had no idea what it meant, may understand him as he intended, because they are able to guess from the context what he was likely to be saying. Moreover, if sufficiently many people make the same mistake, the meaning they wrongly attached to the word may become its meaning in the language. It is a great mistake to conclude from facts like these that a word's meaning is in the first instance bestowed on it by an interior act of the individual speaker. It is only from learning language that anyone acquires the very conception of a word's having a meaning. We do not have meanings in our heads waiting for us to attach them to words, whether of the common language or of our own invention; we learn the *practice* of speaking a language, and learn, in particular, how to form sentences from words and how different words contribute to form sentences that can be used in particular ways. It is from that that we come by the notion of the meanings that different words have. Once we have acquired the practice, we can imitate it by inventing words for private use among friends, or even just in soliloquy; but the fundamental concept is not that of the private meaning-conferring act, but of the social practice of using language.

"The question is", said Alice, "whether you *can* make words mean different things." She picked the right question to ask. We cannot mean whatever we choose by whatever words we elect to utter, even when there is no problem about our having such a meaning in mind, because, say, it is already the meaning of some other word in the language. We cannot *mean* it, not just in the sense that we cannot expect others to understand us, but in the sense that the meaning fuses with the utterance to make our saying it and meaning that by it a unified act, as Husserl required that it should do. Wittgenstein asked the same question as Alice, in a characteristically more subtle way:

> Make the following experiment: *say* "It's cold here" and *mean* "It's warm here". Can you do it? – And what are you doing as you do it? And is there only one way of doing it?[12]

And again:

> Imagine someone pointing to his cheek with an expression of pain and saying "abracadabra!". – We ask "What do you mean?". And he answers "I meant toothache". – You at once think to yourself: How can one '*mean* toothache' by that word? Or what did it *mean* to *mean* pain by the word? And yet, in a different context, you would have asserted that the mental activity of *meaning* such-and-such was just what was most important in the use of language.
>
> But – can't I say "By 'abracadabra' I mean toothache"? Of course I can; but this is a definition; not a description of what goes on in me when I utter the word.[13]

[12] *Philosophical Investigations*, I-510.
[13] Ibid., I-665.

The meaning-conferring act is a myth. Humpty Dumpty's theory was wrong, and Husserl came too close to adopting it. But, even were the meaning-conferring act not a myth, it would answer only the question, "What makes a word to have the particular meaning that it does?" – a question to which, as we saw, Frege had no answer to give – and not the more important question, "What is it for a word to have a meaning?" To this question, Frege had a detailed and rather convincing answer – more detailed and more convincing than any philosopher had offered before him. His answer turned upon his notion of reference: the sense borne by an expression is the way its reference is given to a speaker in virtue of his knowledge of the language.

For Husserl, the significance of a meaningful utterance is due to a mental act that is an ingredient of the composite act of which the physical utterance is the other ingredient. Since the act that confers meaning is a mental act, it must have, or, at worst, purport to have, an object. Husserl was as clear as Frege that two expressions may have different meanings (different senses, in Frege's terminology) but the same objectual reference, giving as one example the pair of definite descriptions "the victor at Jena" and "the loser at Waterloo".[14] Now, on Frege's theory, sense (*Sinn*) determines reference (*Bedeutung*), not merely in the weak sense, alleged by John McDowell to be the only one in which the thesis is true, that no two expressions can have the same sense but different references, but in the stronger sense that, given how things stand in the world independently of language, it is an expression's having the sense that it does that explains what gives it the reference that it has. We can grasp the sense of a name, for example, only if we understand what it is to regard, and to use, an expression as a name, and it refers to the specific object that it does in virtue of the fact that its sense constitutes a particular way of singling out that object. Just as much as did Frege, Husserl regarded the sense of an expression as constituting that in virtue of which it has

[14] *Logische Untersuchungen*, Investigation I, Chapter 1, §12.

whatever objectual reference it has.

> In accordance with these examples we ought to regard the
> distinction between the meaning of an expression and the
> property it has of directing itself as a name to this or that
> objectual correlate (and naturally also the distinction between
> the meaning and the object itself) as assured. It is furthermore
> clear that, for every expression, there obtains a close
> connection between the two sides thus distinguished: namely
> that an expression attains an objectual reference only through
> its meaning what it does, and that it can therefore be rightly
> said that the expression designates (names) the object *in virtue
> of* its meaning, and that the act of meaning is the particular
> way in which we refer to the object at a given time.[15]

Somewhat inconsistently, however, Husserl did not accept the
thesis in what was referred to above as its weak sense: he held
that an expression may have the same meaning, but different
references, in different contexts. Such a view would obviously
be correct for indexical expressions like "here", if "meaning"
were understood as 'linguistic meaning' rather than, like
Frege's "sense", as 'the way the reference is given to the
hearer of the particular utterance'; but Husserl, appealing to
a far more primitive conception of reference than Frege's,
applies it to a general term like "a horse", considered as
predicated of different individual animals.[16]

Given that it is their meanings in virtue of which linguistic
expressions are directed at their objectual referents, can we
not construe Husserl as having an account of the meaning of
an expression in terms of the way its reference is given?
Doubtless we must so construe him; but we cannot derive
from his work any serious rival to Frege's theory. Any account
of meaning must provide an explanation of how the meanings
of expressions of different categories fit together to yield the
meaning of a whole sentence. Frege relied for this on his
notion of an 'unsaturated' or 'incomplete' expression. His
model for such incompleteness was a function, which must be

[15] Ibid., §13.
[16] Ibid., §12.

'completed' by an argument to yield a value. The incompleteness of the linguistic expression consisted, not so much in its being a function, still less in having a function as its sense, but in its having one as its reference. As already remarked, Frege's theory of reference (*Bedeutung*) is meant to serve as an analysis of the process whereby the truth-value of any sentence is determined: determined by reality, as it were, rather than by us, because we may be unable to decide the truth-value. The process is articulated, in a manner corresponding to the articulation of the sentence: the reference of each constituent part is what must be determined in that part of the process corresponding to it. By dint of regarding the references of the 'incomplete' constituents of the sentence as functions of suitable types, the whole process eventuates in the determination, as the value of the sentence, of one of the two values *true* and *false*. The sentence itself must be seen as having a reference, in the light of the fact that it can become a constituent of a more complex sentence: that is why, in 'Über Sinn und Bedeutung', Frege pays so much attention to subordinate clauses. He held that, in a properly constructed language, such as his own symbolic one, a subsentence would contribute to determining the truth-value of the whole only through its own truth-value; in natural language, one may have to interpret the complex sentence as having an additional tacit constituent, indicated by the (grammatical) conjunction, or to take the subordinate clause as having a special, indirect, reference to what would ordinarily be its sense. On the basis of such a well developed account of reference, Frege could represent the sense of each expression, which we grasp, as the way the reference is given to us, and the sense of the sentence as a whole as the thought that the condition for it to have the value *true* is fulfilled.

Frege's theory of reference is thus the foundation of his theory of sense. Since the sense of an expression is in all cases the way in which its reference is given, deciding what, and what kind of thing, constitutes the reference of a given expression is a crucial first step towards characterising its sense, which is required to take the form of a means by which that reference may be given to a speaker of the language. This does not uniquely determine what the sense is to be, but it imposes a powerful constraint on what we may plausibly take it to consist in.[17] The theory of reference thus does not yet constitute a theory of sense, but it does constitute its indispensable foundation: until we have a correct theory of reference, we have no idea of the form that a theory of sense ought to take.

Husserl, too, used the notion of an incomplete expression – one needing completion – to explain the unity of the proposition. In Investigation III he built on the work of Stumpf to frame a much admired theory of the part/whole relation, distinguishing independent (*selbständige*) parts, such as a horse's head, which can be presented in isolation from the whole, from dependent (*unselbständige*) ones, which cannot. In Investigation IV he applied this theory to linguistic expressions. Syncategorematic expressions, such as grammatical conjunctions, are incomplete in any possible sense; but others, such as "larger than a house", are incomplete only in the sense that they have dependent meanings.[18] Frege also regarded the sense of an incomplete expression as itself incomplete; but the only explanation that can be given for his calling it so is that the correlative *reference* is incomplete, as being, not an object, but a function. By contrast, Husserl denied that an expression whose meaning was independent must refer to an independent object; his counter-examples were expressions like "redness".[19] Whereas incompleteness

---

[17] Other constraints are: that the sense must be something that can be grasped; that it must be something of which no fully competent speaker of the language can be ignorant; that any feature ascribed to it must be relevant to determining the reference, so that one who grasped another sense lacking that feature might suppose the reference to differ; that, conversely, everything relevant to determining the reference and involved in understanding the language should be part of the sense; and that a complete account of the sense will fully characterise a piece of knowledge that a speaker has concerning the expression, and will include nothing that, to be a competent speaker, he need not know.

[18] *Logische Untersuchungen*, Investigation IV, §6.

[19] Ibid., §8.

of sense is derived, on Frege's theory, from the incompleteness of the thing referred to, according to a precise semantic account, Husserl debars himself from deriving dependence of meaning in the same way. Frege's strict adherence to his principles led him into paradoxes about expressions like "the concept *horse*";[20] yet in distinguishing "the colour red" and "the number two", as referring to objects, from their adjectival counterparts "... is red" and "... are two", as referring to concepts of first or second level, he saw more clearly than Husserl. As our explanation of how the parts of the sentence fit together, Husserl leaves us with only the highly general idea, *not* part of a theory of how truth-value is determined, of dependent parts of a whole; even his rationale for distinguishing singular terms as having independent meanings is left unstated.

Thus Husserl leaves us with only a vague notion of objectual reference, and only a vague conception of how meaning and objectual reference are related. In deciding what should be reckoned as the reference of an expression, Frege had a precise question to ask: what contribution it made to determining the truth-value of any sentence in which it occurred, where that contribution must be something it had in common with any expression whose substitution for it would in all cases leave the truth-value unaffected. Husserl, by contrast, seems to have had only a rather vague question in mind: what in the world could be taken as corresponding to the expression? He was at no pains to convince anyone that there are, in general, such objectual correlates to all meaningful expressions: the intentionality of mental acts was so axiomatic for him that he perceived no necessity to demonstrate it in particular cases. He therefore lacked any precise theory of the types of reference possessed by different types of expression and of how they fitted together. Indeed, he sometimes writes as though indifferent to what the objectual correlate is taken to be, as long as it is acknowledged that it has one. An instance occurs when he is discussing assertoric sentences. He says:

[20] See G. Frege, 'Über Begriff und Gegenstand' (1892).

If we consider assertoric sentences of the form *S is P*, for example, the object of the statement is normally regarded as being that which constitutes the subject, and thus that *of* which something is asserted. A different conception is, however, also possible, which takes the *whole* state of affairs [*Sachlage*] corresponding to the statement as the analogue of the object denoted by a name and distinguishes it from the meaning of the statement.[21]

The matter is cleared up in Investigation V, where Husserl says:

> ... in the proposition *the knife is on the table*, the knife is indeed the object *about* which we judge or *of* which we are predicating something; at the same time, the knife is not the primary object, that is, the full object of the judgement, but only that of its subject. To the whole judgement there corresponds, as the full and complete object, the *state of affairs* [*Sachverhalt*] judged: identically the same state of affairs can be presented in a presentation, wished for in a wish, asked after in a question, doubted in a doubt, etc.[22]

Thus, like Wittgenstein in the *Tractatus*, Husserl does not follow Frege in taking truth-values as the references of sentences, but, rather, states of affairs. The rather casual attitude to the matter displayed in Investigation I remains a testimony to how comparatively little importance Husserl attached to devising a precise theory of how the parts of a sentence contribute to determining its objectual reference. If we are after a clear theory of linguistic meaning and of linguistic reference, it is to Frege, and not to Husserl, that we must turn.[23]

---

[21] *Logische Untersuchungen*, Investigation I, Chapter 1, §12.
[22] Ibid., Investigation V, Chapter 2, §17.
[23] I have been informed, too late for me to consult it, that Dallas Willard, *Logic and the Objectivity of Knowledge*, Athens, Ohio, 1984, contains an illuminating comparison of Husserl's and Frege's views on meaning.

CHAPTER 7

Sense without Reference

(i) The objects of understanding

G. E. Moore wrote in his commonplace book:

> Can we say that "that thing" = "the thing at which I am pointing" or "the thing to which this finger points" or "the nearest thing to which this finger points"? No, because the prop[osition] is not understood unless the thing in question is seen.[1]

Whether Moore was right in making this claim is here irrelevant: what matters is his use of the term "understood". He is not talking about the understanding of a *sentence*, for instance the sentence, "That thing is in the way", considered as a type. If a teacher of the English language asks his students to translate the sentence, "That thing is in the way" into their language, he is regarding the sentence solely as a type: it would be senseless to ask, "What thing?", or "In the way of what?". When the sentence is considered merely as a type, there is no 'thing in question'; Moore was talking about the understanding of a particular utterance of the sentence – of a serious utterance of it, meaning one used to *say* something and not just by way of referring to the type sentence. Obviously, to understand a particular utterance in

[1] G. E. Moore, *Commonplace Book 1919-1953*, ed. C. Lewy, London, 1962, p. 158; quoted by G. Evans, *Varieties of Reference*, ed. J. McDowell, Oxford, 1982, p. 308n.

57

this sense, it is necessary to understand the type sentence uttered; but Moore clearly held that something more might well be required in order to understand the utterance. He thus recognised a twofold meaning for the verb "to understand": that in which someone is said to understand a word, phrase or sentence, considered as a type, and that in which he may be said to understand a particular utterance. We may call these the 'dispositional' and the 'occurrent' senses of "to understand".

In the celebrated 'On Denoting' in which Russell first expounded his theory of descriptions,[2] he criticised Frege's theory of sense and reference, inaccurately rendering Frege's *Sinn* by his own term "meaning" and Frege's *Bedeutung* by his own term "denotation". In the course of commenting on it, he said:

> If we say "The King of England is bald", that is, it would seem, not a statement about the complex *meaning* 'the King of England', but about the actual man denoted by the meaning. But now consider "the King of France is bald". By parity of form, this also ought to be about the denotation of the phrase "the King of France". But this phrase, though it has a *meaning* provided "the King of England" has a meaning, has certainly no denotation, at least in any obvious sense. Hence one would suppose that "The King of France is bald" ought to be nonsense; but it is not nonsense, since it is plainly false.

Frege would not have said that the sentence was nonsense, but that it had a sense, and so expressed a thought. But he would also not have said that it was false, since he would have regarded the absence of a reference for the constituent "the King of France" as depriving the whole of reference, and thus of truth-value; the thought expressed was neither true nor false.

Strawson, in his well-known attack on Russell's theory of

---

[2] B. Russell, 'On Denoting', *Mind*, n.s., Vol. 14, 1905, pp. 479-93; reprinted in B. Russell, *Essays in Analysis*, ed. D. Lackey, London, 1973, and in many other places.

descriptions,[3] accused Russell of confusing two different subjects to which the predications "true"/"false" and "meaningful"/"nonsensical" could be applied. According to him, it is only of *sentences* that we can say that they are meaningful or meaningless, whereas it is of *assertions* or of particular *uses* of sentences that we say that they are true or false. He makes it clear that an occasion of utterance is essential to a use of a sentence, and affects what assertion was made by it: by the utterance of one and the same sentence on different occasions, by different speakers or the same one, different assertions may be made. It is equally plain that he is understanding the term "sentence" solely in the sense of a *type*. He is thus treating "meaningful" and "meaningless" as applicable only to sentences considered as types, and not to specific utterances. But something may be said to be meaningful just in case it can be understood; Strawson is therefore confining "understand" to its dispositional sense.

Inasmuch as it is used to mean 'the *present* King of France', the phrase "the King of France" has an indexical element. In his reply to Strawson,[4] Russell points out that the problem of empty definite descriptions does not arise solely for sentences involving indexicality. There is, however, a converse point to be made: that understanding does *not* relate solely to sentence-types, but also to particular utterances. An utterance is meaningful just in case it can be understood, which means: understood as *saying* something. It is meaningful, therefore, if and only if it does *say* something. Frege called what is expressed by a sentence a "thought", and held that truth and falsity are predicated of thoughts absolutely: a thought could not, for him, be true at one time and false at another, or true for one subject and false for another, but is simply true or simply false. It is plain that a thought cannot in general be what a type sentence expresses, but what is

[3] P. F. Strawson, 'On Referring', *Mind*, n.s., Vol. 59, 1950, pp. 320-44; reprinted with additional footnotes in A. Flew (ed.), *Essays in Conceptual Analysis*, London, 1956, and again in P. F. Strawson, *Logico-Linguistic Papers*, London, 1971.

[4] 'Mr. Strawson on Referring', *Mind*, n.s., Vol. 66, 1957, pp. 385-9.

expressed by a particular utterance of a sentence; and anyone who so uses a term like "proposition" or "statement" as referring to what is true or false absolutely must hold the same. And this entails the recognition of an occurrent sense of "understand": to understand a particular utterance will involve grasping the thought or proposition it expresses.

We need an occurrent sense of "understand" for two reasons: indexicality and ambiguity. The problem addressed by Moore in the quotation given above is how much is needed in order to understand, in the occurrent sense, an utterance involving indexicality. If, for example, I hear someone say "There is a sinister smell here", how much do I need to know about where he is to know what statement he was making or what thought he was expressing, in that sense under which, if true, it is true absolutely? But ambiguity also calls for an occurrent sense of "understand". If someone utters an ambiguous sentence, his hearers may understand it in a particular way, whether as he intended or not; we may speak also, not only of how the speaker meant it, but of how he was understanding it.

It is in view of his having, in effect, simply dismissed the occurrent sense of "understand" that Evans judges that Strawson "failed to join issue with Russell in any effective way".[5] Russell's problem is to explain how the utterance of a sentence containing an empty definite description can nevertheless say something. If it does not say anything, the utterance will be meaningless and cannot be understood in the occurrent sense, even though the *sentence*, considered as a type, may be meaningful. Strawson does not face this issue, but, in effect, rules it out of order by laying down that "meaningful" and "meaningless" can properly be applied only to sentence-types. Frege's solution, which Evans rightly finds intolerable, is to allow that such an utterance does, in one sense, say something, namely that it expresses a thought; in another, it says nothing because it does not succeed even in being false (let alone true).

What makes Frege's solution intolerable is not the claim that

---

[5] G. Evans, op. cit., p. 52n.

the utterance of a sentence containing an empty name or description nevertheless expresses a thought, but the denial to that thought of a truth-value. In his writings after 'On Referring', Strawson took to using the expression "does not make a statement, true or false". This is of course ambiguous between "makes a statement, which is not either true or false" and "fails to make a statement". Frege's option was the former; but the word "false" does not have the power to give us an idea of what it is to say something that is not even false, unless it be to fail to say anything at all. To say something in circumstances that do not satisfy the condition for what is said to be true *is*, in a clear sense of "false", to say something false. Frege denied this in consequence of construing too literally his identification of truth-values as the references of sentences. If there is no such country as Ruritania, so that the name "Ruritania" lacks reference, then there is no such city as the capital of Ruritania, so that the phrase "the capital of Ruritania" lacks a reference: if the part lacks reference, the whole must lack reference. Applying the analogy mechanically yields the result that, if "the King of France" lacks a reference, "The King of France is bald" must lack a reference; since the reference of a sentence is a truth-value, "The King of France is bald" must lack a truth-value. But the conclusion lacks any intuitive justification. The logic and semantics of a language in which it is possible to form singular terms lacking a denotation must necessarily be more complex than the purely classical logic and two-valued semantics of Frege's formal language; but that does not warrant the *philosophical* contention that, although the condition for the truth of a sentence containing such a term is well defined, and the sentence therefore expresses a thought, still it lacks a truth-value altogether.

(ii) Gaps in explanation

A thought, for Frege, is a timeless object. It may be grasped by different individuals on different occasions, and expressed in different ways; it thus corresponds to Husserl's 'ideal meaning'. A speaker expresses a certain thought, and the hearer will take him as expressing a certain thought; if he is not misunderstanding, it will be the same thought. But, though Frege repeatedly states that the thought is the sense of the sentence, it cannot be identified with the meaning of the sentence considered as a type, for the same two reasons as before. If the sentence contains an overtly or tacitly indexical expression, the thought expressed by the speaker's utterance of it will be in part determined by non-linguistic features of the context; if it is ambiguous, it will be determined by his intention.

Frege insisted that, in contrast to what he called 'ideas' (*Vorstellungen*) – the components of the stream of consciousness – thoughts and their constituent senses are objective. Unlike the equally objective denizens of the physical world, however, they are not actual (*wirklich*): they are not subject to change, and do not act causally upon other objects. They are therefore neither contents of the mind nor located in space and time within the external world: they inhabit a 'third realm'. When the matter is so expressed, a problem appears to arise about our apprehension of these objective but non-actual entities; and, in a notorious passage in one of his uncompleted and unpublished attempts to compose a book on philosophical logic, Frege gave voice to perplexity about it:

> ... the law of gravitation ... is completely independent of everything which takes place in my brain and of every change or alteration in my ideas. But grasping this law is nevertheless a mental process! Yes: but a process that lies at the very boundary of the mental and can accordingly not be completely understood from a purely psychological standpoint. For in it something comes into account that is no longer mental in the proper sense: the thought; and perhaps this process is the most mysterious of all.[6]

What Frege here calls 'the most mysterious process of all' is the mental act of grasping a thought. From the standpoint of his mythology of the third realm, it indeed appears

[6] G. Frege, 'Logik' (1897), *Posthumous Writings*, p. 145.

mysterious. We perceive physical objects by means of our senses, and perceive them always in some particular way; by one or another sense-modality, by means of this or that sense-organ, from a certain distance, in a certain direction, in particular physical circumstances. But with what organ do we grasp a thought? It cannot be presented to you and to me in different ways: if you grasped it in one way and I in another, the way each of us grasped it would be part of the sense, and hence it would not be precisely the same thought that we both grasped.

This is what Barry Smith refers to as the 'linkage problem'.[7] The problem is to characterise the tie between thoughts and cognitive activities: between thoughts, considered as objective, immutable entities – 'ideal unities', in Husserl's term – and those of our mental acts whose contents they are. Smith claims that, while Frege's theory fails to solve this problem, Husserl's succeeds. For Husserl, the ideal meaning is a species of which the individual act is a member: no tighter link than instantiation can be found, Smith urges.

But does Frege really face such a problem? When he was writing his uncompleted 'Logik', he thought he did: but did he really? When the matter is viewed through the imagery of the third realm, it indeed appears acute. But when we come down to earth, and consider the expression of thoughts in language, it evaporates. Frege believed that the only access we human beings have to thoughts is through their verbal expression; so the question how we grasp thoughts resolves into the question how we understand sentences. Of that, Frege appears to have a theory that dissolves the mystery, at least as far as our grasp of that aspect of meaning he calls 'sense' is concerned. The sense of an expression is the way its reference is given to us; the references of the words in a sentence together serve to determine its truth-value, so that to grasp the thought it expresses is to grasp the condition for it to be true. The mystery has vanished; indeed, the third realm has vanished, too.

[7] B. Smith, 'On the Origins of Analytic Philosophy', *Grazer philosophische Studien*, Vol. 35, 1989, pp. 163 and 169.

That is not to say that no gap remains. As already remarked, Frege's insistence on the objectivity of thoughts themselves provides no guarantee that our attachment to the words of a language of the senses that they bear is objective. The problem is not to explain how we attach particular senses to them: that is accounted for in terms of Frege's theory of the relation of sense to reference and of his notion of reference. The problem is how it can be objectively ascertained that two speakers attach the same senses to the words they use. There is also a gap between the apprehension of sense and the practice of using the language: the conventions that confer upon the utterance of one or another sentence expressing a given thought the significance it has for us. And these two gaps are one. Once an explanation is forthcoming of the connection between our recognition of the condition for a sentence to be true, in accordance with Frege's theory of sense, and the use we make of that sentence, we can describe the means whereby one speaker can determine whether or not another associates the same truth-condition with it as he, namely by the way in which he uses it.

Frege's explanations *can* start with language; indeed, if they are not to run headlong into Smith's 'linkage problem', they *must* start with language. That, as we have seen, is not to say that sense can always be simply identified with linguistic meaning. If senses are constituents of thoughts that are true or false absolutely, they cannot be so identified for those many words of a language which have distinct senses in identifiably different contexts; nor for those words properly termed 'ambiguous', which may bear one or another sense in the same context. Equivocity, of either degree, is no great problem for an account of linguistic meaning in accordance with Frege's theory of sense; but sense obviously comes apart from linguistic meaning for indexical terms like "now", "I" and so on. Less obviously, the two come apart, on Frege's theory, for words in indirect speech, which obviously retain their ordinary linguistic meaning, but, according to Frege, do not have their ordinary reference, referring instead to what are ordinarily their senses. Since their reference is different, their senses must be, too, Frege argues, since sense determines reference; and, when we view sense as the way the reference is given, the argument is clearly sound.

The linguistic meaning of an indexical term evidently contributes to the sense it expresses on a particular occasion of utterance. This is not merely to state the obvious fact that, if someone does not know what "now" means in the language, he will not know what thought is expressed by the utterance of a sentence containing that word; for even if he cannot understand that sentence, he might be able to grasp the thought, for instance if he understood some other sentence, in the same or another language, that expressed it. It is, rather, that he *must* have some equivalent means of expressing it; he must be able to think of the time referred to as that which includes the present moment, and, to do that, he must be able to indicate that moment as the present one. To know what thought is expressed by a sentence containing an indexical term, the hearer must know the semantic rule determining the reference of the term from the context; for instance, that the first-person pronoun "I" refers to the speaker, and the second-person pronoun "you" to the person addressed. It is an illusion, however, to suppose that it is enough to state this rule in order to explain the sense a speaker or hearer attaches to an utterance of the term. The sense is the way the reference is *given* to the subject; and so an account is needed of how a subject identifies the reference in accordance with the semantic rule, and what it is to identify it in that way.[8] Husserl indeed says something very similar:

> From one occasion to another the word "I" names a different person, and does this by means of an ever-changing meaning ... But the conceptual presentation it evokes is not the meaning of the word "I". Otherwise we could simply substitute for "I" the phrase "the speaker who is presently designating

---

[8] For a detailed discussion of this point, in the light of a controversy between Gareth Evans and John Perry, see M. Dummett, 'The Relative Priority of Thought and Language', in *Frege and Other Philosophers*, Oxford, 1991.

himself" ... It is the general *meaning-function* of the word "I" to designate the present speaker, but the concept through which we express this function is not the concept which immediately and of itself constitutes its meaning.[9]

Husserl's "general meaning-function" is referred to above as the semantic rule.

In order to explain the sense a speaker or hearer attaches to an utterance of an indexical term, it is not enough to state the semantic rule that governs it. Indeed, it is incorrect to claim that, to grasp the thought which may be expressed by a sentence containing the term, it is necessary to conceive of an expression governed by just that rule. A child does not need to have mastered the use of the first-person pronoun in order to be able to have thoughts concerning himself, as one person among others: he may use his own name in speaking of himself to others or in thinking of himself. To conceive of that as his *name*, however, he must have names for other people, and therefore a way of asking after their names ("Who is that?"). He could therefore ask after his own name if he were to be afflicted by amnesia, perhaps by saying "Who is this?"; this would be his equivalent of "Who am I?", in which case "this", in that use, is governed by the same semantic rule as governs "I" for an adult. On the other hand, if the child does not conceive of what adults think of as his name as a name, then it is, in his mouth, the first-person pronoun. But only in his mouth: it is *not* for him, governed by the rule that, in the mouth of each speaker, it refers to that speaker: it refers, in everyone's mouth, to *him*. What makes it, nevertheless, a pronoun rather than a name is that it is not, for the child, an answer to the question who he is: either he does not know any other names, and so has not the concept of a name, or it does not occur to him that others may not know the word he uses to refer to himself (and they think of as his name).

Linguistic meaning is not to be identified with sense; but, if one starts from language, there is no obstacle in principle to giving an account of sense on the basis of linguistic meaning.

[9] *Logische Untersuchungen*, Investigation I, Chapter 3, §26.

Husserl, however, starts from the other end. He starts from the content of the individual mental act. From there he ascends to the 'ideal meaning' as the species to which it belongs. So far, language has played no part, even if the act is an expressive one, in which the mental act is fused with a linguistic utterance. And here is the gap in Husserl's theory: how are the meanings attached to the words? What renders those words an *expression* of the meaning? After all, when the act is one of judgement, say, the meaning-components of the complete judgement cannot in all cases be identified with the linguistic meanings: so how are words and meaning related? Where is the difficulty? – it may be asked. After all, if it is primarily indexical expressions – what Husserl calls 'essentially occasional' expressions – that compel us to distinguish thought-constituents from linguistic meanings, Husserl treats of these quite successfully. That, however, is not the problem, at least not the major problem, which is far more general. If we already have a conception of the ideal meaning which informs the act, our explanation of the significance of linguistic items must make use of this if the explanations are not to be given all over again a second time: it must appeal to some notion of 'expression' which will connect the words, phrases and sentences with those ideal meanings. Language now appears, not as the vehicle of the meaning, but merely as an instrument for transmitting it; expression can be explained only as encoding. If such an account could be made to work, language would be, from a philosophical standpoint, of quite secondary importance. As we shall see, it cannot be made to work.

The relation between a sense or meaning as a constituent of a proposition that can be grasped by different people and expressed repeatedly and as involved in a particular act of thinking is not that of type to token, or of universal to instance: the individual act *exploits* the general meaning. Mathematicians do not, for example, first have various thoughts involving the concept of integration, and then arrive at the meaning of the integral sign, or at the general concept, by noticing what is in common between all these individual thoughts. Rather, having first learned what integration is and how to use the sign of integration in equations, they proceed to use it in confidence that any feature of its proper use will be available to them when it is needed: only when they had learned the meaning of the sign were they able to have the thoughts they use it to express. "When we use the word 'integral', for example, are we then always conscious of everything that belongs to the sense of this word?", Frege asked in a lecture to mathematics students,[10] and continued, "I believe we do so only in rare cases. Usually only the word is in our consciousness, coupled, indeed, with the more or less dim knowledge that this word is a sign that has a sense, and that we can remember this sense when we wish to." There is something we could call 'bearing the sense of the word "integral" in mind', namely remaining conscious of its definition; but when I say, "Thank you for taking so much trouble", it scarcely makes sense to ask whether I am bearing the meaning of the word "trouble" in mind. The linguistic meaning comes first. We learn how to use the words of our language, and proceed so to use them: we do not impart a ready-made meaning to our words, and subsequently partition these imparted meanings into equivalence types. In at least the overwhelming majority of cases, we could not have the thought unless we had first been given the word, or some synonymous word; once given the word, we need do nothing more in order to mean by it what it means than to use it.

(iii) Failure of reference

For Husserl, as for Frege after 1890, the distinction between meaning and objectual reference renders unproblematic the existence of meaningful expressions which miss their mark by lacking any objectual correlate. We have to distinguish between lack of reference and meaninglessness, even between being logically contradictory and being meaningless, for, if we do not, we cannot explain the meaningfulness of a (true)

---

[10] 'Logik in der Mathematik' (1914), *Posthumous Writings*, p. 209.

denial of existence.

Some have found unconvincing the claim that a distinction between sense and reference makes it possible to acknowledge the existence of terms with sense but without reference. For example, in an early phase, both Evans and McDowell argued that, if the sense is the way in which the referent is given to us, then, if there is no referent, there can be no way in which it is given, and hence no sense. Evans came to abandon this simple argument; McDowell has remained more faithful to it.[11] Although strongly opposed to the 'direct reference' school which wants to dispense with the notion of sense altogether, at least for singular terms, Evans continued to believe that a great many singular terms are what he called 'Russellian': that is, incapable of having the kind of sense they appear to have, and hence of having a sense at all, if an object is lacking. Indeed, his posthumous book was largely devoted to exploring Russellian terms and the corresponding ways of thinking about objects.[12] The price of holding such a view is to be compelled to concede that we are not always aware whether an expression has a sense or not; if there is no object referred to by some given Russellian term, the term lacks a sense, even though no means is available to us of knowing that it does. If a term lacks a sense, a sentence in which it is used will lack a sense, also: such a sentence will not express a thought, and one who utters it will not have succeeded in *saying* anything. It follows that, through no fault of his own, a subject may suppose himself to have a thought, or to have expressed it, when in fact there is no such thought to be had.

Nevertheless, Evans did not regard being Russellian as a defining characteristic of a singular term. No one could do so who classified definite descriptions as singular terms. In common with the 'direct reference' school, however, Evans did not so classify them, on the ground that, unlike proper names, they do not behave, in modal and temporal contexts, as having a fixed reference. He therefore adopted Russell's theory of

[11] See, e.g., John McDowell, 'On the Sense and Reference of a Proper Name', *Mind*, n.s., Vol. 86, 1977, pp. 159-85.
[12] G. Evans, op. cit.

descriptions, in a form without "the butchering of surface structure in which Russell so perversely delighted".[13] Despite this, he was at pains to point out the existence of a small class of proper names whose references are fixed by definite descriptions, but whose behaviour in modal and temporal contexts does not impugn their status as singular terms; for example, "deutero-Isaiah", whose reference is given as the author of the second part of the book of Isaiah. Such a 'descriptive name' is not Russellian. Even if such a name lacks a reference, because it happens that nothing answers the description, that fact does not deprive it of sense: one who utters a sentence containing it *says* something – expresses a thought, which must, therefore, have a truth-value. Frege's own conclusion that, while expressing a thought, it would lack a truth-value, arose, as Evans saw, from his strict identification of the semantic value of a singular term with the object to which it serves to refer; Frege drew no distinction between reference and semantic value, his term *"Bedeutung"* serving both purposes. Evans's contrary view may be expressed by the compelling slogan "No sense without a semantic value". The price of accepting it is to have to allow that a non-Russellian singular term that lacks a reference still has a semantic value, consisting in the bare fact of its lack of reference.

At no stage of his philosophical evolution did Husserl have any qualms on this point: it seemed evident to him that an expression may have a sense even if it lacks an objectual reference. His fundamental thought, in the period following the *Logische Untersuchungen*, was that the notion of sense could be generalised from expressive acts to all mental acts: for the generalised notion, he used the term "noema". The correct interpretation of the notion of noema, first introduced in the *Ideen* of 1913,[14] has been the most fiercely contested in

[13] Ibid., p. 57.

[14] *Ideen zu einer reinen Phänomenologie und phänomenologischen Philosophie*, Vol. I, in *Jahrbuch für Philosophie und phänomenologische Forschung*, Vol. 1, 1913, pp. 1-323; reprinted Tübingen, 1980, and, as Vol. III of *Husserliana*, ed. W. Biemel, in the Hague, 1950. English trans. by

the burgeoning exegetical literature on Husserl. Herman Philipse maintains that it marked a shift in his conception of intentionality: where he had previously denied intentionality to be a relation, he now accepted it as such, and took the noema as the end-term of that relation.[15] Philipse uneasily asks "why there are so many texts which seem to support" an interpretation under which the noema is not on the object side of intention, and replies that the concepts of "intentionality and noema have an ambivalent nature, due to the fact that Husserl used them in solving problems in fields so different as perception and semantics".[16] It may indeed be questioned whether any one concept can be applied univocally both to sense-perception and to linguistic significance; but to maintain that Husserl wavered over the question whether a noema is or is not the object to which our mental acts are directed is surely to attribute to him a degree of confusion incompatible with his meriting serious attention as a philosopher. In support of his interpretation, Philipse cites *Ideen*, §88; but, aware as I am that Philipse has studied Husserl far more closely than I, I cannot see that the section demands, or even admits of, so radical a construction:

> Let us suppose that we are looking with pleasure in a garden at a blossoming apple-tree, at the fresh young green of the lawn, and so forth. The perception and the pleasure that accompanies it are obviously not that which at the same time is perceived and gives pleasure.... Let us now pass over to the phenomenological standpoint. The transcendent world enters its "bracket"; we activate the ἐποχή in relation to its actual existence.... Here in regard to the perception, ... we have no such question to put as whether anything corresponds to it in

W. R. Boyce Gibson, *Ideas: a General Introduction to Pure Phenomenology*, London, 1931, and as *Ideas pertaining to a pure Phenomenology and to a phenomenological Philosophy* by F. Kersten, Dordrecht, 1982. This was the only volume published in Husserl's lifetime: Volumes II and III were published as Volumes IV and V of *Husserliana*, again ed. W. Biemel, in 1952. The unqualified title *Ideen* will here refer only to the first volume.

[15] H. Philipse, 'The Concept of Intentionality: Husserl's Development from the Brentano Period to the *Logical Investigations*', *Philosophy Research Archives*, Vol. XII, 1986-7, pp. 293-328.

[16] Ibid., note 66.

"reality".... This reality, by the standard of our judgement, is simply not there for us, nor, likewise, anything that needs positing or accepting in relation to this posited or accepted reality. And yet everything remains, so to speak, as of old. Even the phenomenologically reduced perceptual experience is a perception *of* "this apple-tree in bloom, in this garden, and so forth", and likewise the reduced pleasure, a pleasure in the thing itself.

The reduction of ἐποχή is the celebrated 'bracketing' of transcendent reality: prescinding from the existence or constitution of the external world, we attend solely to the mental act, indifferent to whether its object exists or not. Husserl's point is that, even when we adopt this purely phenomenological attitude, the intentional character of the act remains unaltered: the perception is still a perception *of* an apple-tree, the pleasure is still pleasure *in* the beauty of the apple-tree. But this no more implies that the noema, which is that to which the act owes its intentional character, has now become the object of an intentional relation than Frege's admitting that a term may have a sense but lack an objectual reference implies that in such a case it refers to its sense. In the sentence "Etna is higher than Vesuvius", Frege wrote,

> we have the proper name "Etna", which makes a contribution to the sense of the whole sentence, to the thought. This contribution is a part of the thought; it is the sense of the word "Etna". But we are not predicating anything of this sense, but of a mountain, which is not part of the thought. An epistemological idealist may now say, "That is a mistake. Etna is only your idea." Anyone who utters the sentence "Etna is higher than Vesuvius" understands it in the sense that in it something is to be predicated of an object that is quite independent of the speaker. The idealist may now say that it is a mistake to take the name "Etna" as designating anything. In that case the speaker is lost in the realm of fable and fiction, whereas he believes that he is moving in the realm of truth. The idealist is not justified, however, in so turning the thought round as to make the speaker designate by the name "Etna"

one of his ideas and report something about that. Either the speaker designates by the name "Etna" what he wants to designate, or he designates nothing by the name, which is then without reference.[17]

Save in the special case of its occurring within indirect speech, Frege would object equally to the proposal that, when a term lacked an objectual reference, it then designated its sense. It is in virtue of its sense that a name like "Etna" is directed towards an object: its sense *is* the route to the object. If it misses its mark – if there is no object at the place at which it is aimed – it still has the quality of being directed at an object, or, rather, as at an object, but, because there is no such object, it lacks a reference: it does not acquire its sense as an unintended object.

The same surely holds for Husserl's notion of noema. "Each intentional experience has a noema and in it a sense through which it relates to the object", he wrote, and again, "Every noema has a '*content*', namely its '*sense*', and is related through it to 'its' *object*."[18] Here the noema is clearly distinguished from the object; it is not itself the object, but, like Frege's *Sinn*, that through which the act relates to the object. This is the interpretation for which Dagfinn Føllesdal has repeatedly argued, and which is supported by Ronald McIntyre and David Woodruff Smith;[19] since it appears to

[17] 'Logik in der Mathematik', *Posthumous Writings*, p. 232.
[18] *Ideen*, §§135, 129.
[19] D. Føllesdal, 'Husserl's Notion of Noema', *Journal of Philosophy*, Vol. 66, 1969, pp. 680-7, reprinted in Hubert L. Dreyfus (ed.), *Husserl, Intentionality and Cognitive Science*, Cambridge, Massachusetts, 1982; R. McIntyre and D. Woodruff Smith, 'Husserl's Identification of Meaning and Noema', also in H. L. Dreyfus (ed.), op. cit., and *Husserl and Intentionality*, Dordrecht, 1982, Chap. IV. The older interpretation, according to which a noema could be said to be perceived, is expounded in Dorion Cairns, 'An Approach to Phenomenology', in M. Farber (ed.), *Essays in Memory of Edmund Husserl*, Cambridge., Mass., 1940, and in Aron Gurwitsch, *The Field of Consciousness*, Pittsburgh, 1964, and *Studies in Phenomenology and Psychology*, Evanston, 1966. For an attempt at an eclectic view, see Robert C. Solomon, 'Husserl's Concept of the Noema', in F. A. Elliston and P. McCormick (eds.), *Husserl: Expositions and Appraisals*, Notre Dame, 1977. Barry Smith, in his critical notice of *Ursprünge der analytischen*

accord with Husserl's words, it will, with all respect to Herman Philipse, be followed here.

On this interpretation, then, the notion of a noema is a generalisation of that of sense to all mental acts, that is, to all acts or states possessing the characteristic of intentionality.[20] The object of any mental act is given through its noema: the noema is intrinsically directed towards an object, and it is therefore their possession of a noema that accounts for the intentionality of mental acts. Just as with sense, it is in virtue of the noema that an act has whatever object it has. Husserl's new notion of the noema embraces both what, in the *Logische Untersuchungen*, he had called 'matter' and 'quality', where these correspond respectively to what Frege called 'sense' and 'force'; but, without being fully consistent, Husserl tends to restrict the term 'sense' to what tallies with 'matter', thus increasing the similarity between his use of it and Frege's.

By means of the distinction between the object of a mental act and its noema, Husserl sought a final resolution of Brentano's problem. Every mental act must have a noema, and hence must have the quality of being directed towards an object: but it is no more problematic that there should be a noema that misses its mark, so that no external object corresponds to it, than that a linguistic expression should have a sense that fails to supply it, the world being as it is, with any actual objectual reference. A delusive perception is therefore no longer a problem: it possesses the feature of intentionality as well as does a veridical one, but simply happens to lack any actual object.

Philosophie, already cited, assumes "for present purposes" that Føllesdal's interpretation is correct (fn. 12), without actually endorsing it.

[20] "We must everywhere take the noematic correlate, which, in a very extended meaning of the term, is here referred to as sense (*Sinn*), precisely as it lies 'immanent' in the experience of perception, of judgement, of liking, and so forth" (*Ideen*, §88). "The noema is nothing but a generalisation of the idea of meaning to the entire domain of acts" (*Ideen*, Volume III, §3, p. 89) – a favourite quotation of Føllesdal's. In *Ideen*, Husserl was disposed to use the word *Sinn* where, in the *Logische Untersuchungen*, he had used *Bedeutung*. He avows this intention in *Ideen*, §124, after first remarking that the meaning of "*Bedeutung*" must be extended so as to be applied "to all acts, … whether these are interwoven with expressive acts or not".

This is, at least initially, highly plausible: it seems clear, in fact, that some solution along these general lines has to be adopted. Less clear is Husserl's claim that the theory guards against the idealist dilemma. He had insisted that the meaning of the words employed in a linguistic act is not, in the standard case, an object of our thought. "In the act of meaning the meaning is not present to consciousness as an object", he had said in *Logische Untersuchungen* and, further: "if we perform the act, and live in it, as it were, we naturally refer to its object and not to its meaning".[21] Frege only very occasionally discussed what we are conscious of when we are speaking, considering this irrelevant to the objective properties of our words – their senses and their references; but he of course distinguished sharply between the normal case, when we are speaking of the ordinary referent of an expression, and the special one, in which we are speaking of what is ordinarily its sense. In the same spirit, Husserl maintained that we genuinely perceive the objects of our acts of perception; this is not a mere manner of speaking, to cover the real truth that it is the noemata that we directly apprehend. On the contrary, the noema does not normally play the role of an object of the observer's awareness at all, still less of his perceptions. Just as, in the normal case, a speaker is talking and thinking about the *objectual referent* of his utterance, and not about the meaning in virtue of which the utterance has that reference, so a perceiver perceives an object in virtue of the noema of his act or perception, and does not perceive or otherwise apprehend that noema.

Husserl's theory is thus distinguished from a sense-datum theory, as ordinarily understood, according to which sense-data *are* the primary objects of awareness. In the case of perception, too, Husserl thought that we *can*, by an act of reflection, make the noema the object of our attention: but he held in this case that this is an extraordinarily difficult thing to do, which only the philosopher can achieve, and that it is the fundamental task of philosophy to fasten attention on noemata and attain a characterisation of them.

[21] *Logische Untersuchungen*, Investigation I, Chap. 4, §34.

CHAPTER 8

Noemata and Idealism

Husserl's contention that the noema/object distinction blocks the idealist slide is far from evident. On the contrary, it is in danger of beginning it. That is the view of Barry Smith, who applauds my having maintained this in *Ursprünge der analytischen Philosophie*, but argues the point from a slightly different perspective.[1] The introduction of noemata, Smith argues, reinstates the 'linkage problem'. Noemata, he says, "are seen as intermediaries, falling (somehow) *between* the act and its (putative) object". This is unfair, it may be replied: no more than a Fregean sense does a Husserlian noema stand between an act and its object; it is the *way to* the object. The one theory no more threatens an idealist conclusion than does the other: to think that it does, its defender may argue, is to be influenced by the merely historical fact that Husserl finished as a transcendental idealist, while Frege remained the stoutest of realists all his life. We can evaluate this objection only when we have enquired whether, despite his own realist convictions, Frege's theory may be suspected of courting the danger of an idealist conclusion.

Philipse, too, is emphatically of the opinion that the introduction of the noema, which, in his view, involved a transformation of Husserl's conception of intentionality, "was one of the many steps on [his] 'long and thorny' road towards transcendental idealism".[2] In the last chapter we rejected the

[1] B. Smith, op. cit., p. 169.
[2] H. Philipse, op. cit., p. 317.

76

interpretation of the notion of noemata favoured by Philipse, preferring to side with the opposite camp, of which Føllesdal is the best known champion. Faced with a tussle between opposed opinions, there are four things one can do, apart from ignoring the question. One can side with one camp or the other; one can occupy the middle ground, declaring both sides to be partially right; or one can condemn both sides as in error. Concerning the interpretation of the noema, Robert Solomon adopts the reconciliatory strategy; making a point on the side of Gurwitsch's interpretation, and against Føllesdal's, he quotes Husserl as characterising the perceptual noema as "the perceived as such",[3] and comments that "an unquestionable absurdity seems to arise when one suggests that the 'perceived as such' is not itself perceived".[4] David Bell, on the other hand, adopts the fourth strategy in its most satisfying form, ascribing the *same* error to the opposing parties.[5] An instance of this error is to construe a phrase like "the perceived as such" or "the intended as intended" as a singular term referring to some special kind of object. On the contrary, Bell says, to ascribe some property to 'the perceived as such' is simply to ascribe that property to what is perceived, and to reckon it as having that property in virtue of its being perceived. Likewise, the term "noema" itself relates to whatever makes an experience significant. We may justifiably ask, of any given experience, what makes it significant; the subordinate clause here is a legitimate indirect question, to be answered by citing whatever features of the experience distinguish it from an experience lacking that significance. But both sides in the dispute over the interpretation of the concept of a noema make, in effect, the same unwarranted presumption, on Bell's view. This presumption is that the phrase "what makes the experience significant" denotes some object; the two schools differ only over what it denotes. On the contrary, Bell argues, that phrase is a spurious singular term, which does not denote

[3] *Ideen*, §§88, 90.
[4] Robert C. Solomon, op. cit., p. 175, right-hand column.
[5] David Bell, *Husserl*, pp. 179-81.

anything. The concept of a noema is not a genuine sortal
concept, he declares, but just a ragbag concept into which
heterogeneous items can be thrown all of which contribute to
the significance of this or that experience or act.

All this is rather convincing: but it convinces us, at best, of
what Husserl *ought* to have said or meant, not of what he *did*
mean. How could even Husserl, if he meant what Bell claims,
have written, "We can and must put the question of essence:
*What is the 'perceived as such'? What essential phases does it
harbour within itself in its capacity as noema?*"?[6] But, to
whatever extent Bell is right, his point does not render our
question vacuous. For it is unquestionably Husserl's doctrine
that one component of a noema is a sense, where "sense" is
construed narrowly to correspond to "matter" in the earlier
terminology, and so in a manner closely akin to Frege's
understanding of the term, but generalised so as to apply to
all intentional acts, perception included. Even if *noema* is a
ragbag concept, *sense* is not: not, at least, under any
acceptable interpretation of the word. We are therefore still
faced with the question: can the distinction between noema
and object block a slide into idealism?

Certainly, it may be said against the imputation of any
idealistic tendency, if there exists an object of a perceptual act
in reality, then, according to Husserl's theory, what the
subject perceives is that real object. Moreover, we cannot say
that he perceives it only indirectly, on the ground that the
object is mediated by the noema: for there is no notion of
direct perception to which we could contrast it. In just the
same manner, every object must, for both Kant and Frege, be
given to us in a particular way: but we cannot say on this
ground that, for them, objects are only ever given to us
indirectly, since the notion of an object's being given, but not
in any particular way, is on their view incoherent; nothing can
be called indirect unless something more direct is at least
conceivable.

All the same, if each mental act could have the noema that

6 *Ideen*, end of §88.

it has without there being any external object, the sceptical question must arise with what right we assume that there are any external objects at all. The reply might be that, since it is integral to the noema that it purports to be directed towards an external object, we have no option but to take ourselves as perceiving such an object, save in those cases in which contrary evidence compels us to suppress our natural inclination; hence, whenever we really do perceive an object, we may rightly be said to know that the object is there, in virtue of our perceiving it. The sceptic will obviously be equal to this manoeuvre: he may allow that, in such a case, we know that the object is present, but replace his question how we know that by the question how we know that we know it. The situation is unaltered if we adopt the strategy employed by Evans for a large range of singular terms, about which he holds that, if there is no object, they cannot have a sense, though we may suppose that they have: the sceptic's question will still be how we ever know that we know that we are referring to or thinking of any object.

Admittedly, it would be harder, from a Husserlian standpoint, to make the idealist's response to the sceptic, which consists in embracing his doubts but declaring them misplaced, since what they call in question was spurious from the outset. For Berkeley, common sense is uninfected by delusion: it does not endorse the conception of independently existing material bodies which are the causes of our sensory ideas. That conception is, indeed, incoherent, but, according to him, it is no part of common sense, but only an invention of philosophers. It would be much harder to maintain an analogous position in respect of Husserlian noemata, since it is intrinsic to them, as to Fregean senses, to be means by which external objects appear to be given to us, and so to point beyond themselves. If an expression has no reference, we may still, on Frege's view, grasp its sense, and suffer no illusion simply by doing so; but no judgement we make in which that sense is a constituent can be true. Likewise, if there were no external objects, we should not, from Husserl's standpoint, be subject to error if we were able to observe the world in a

non-committal spirit, like one unsure whether he is awake or
dreaming: but, since our perceptions are, to use a phrase
beloved of Christopher Peacocke, always as of objects in
three-dimensional space existing independently of those
perceptions, the natural and primordial manner of perception
is suffused with judgements that those objects are as we
perceive them to be. We cannot know that the sceptic is
wrong: but we can be sure that, if he is right, our error is not
due either to the perversity of philosophers or to the
coarseness of common sense, but to the fact that our
experience is intrinsically misleading. For all that, however,
such a conclusion is not ruled out by the theory of noemata: it
would merely constitute a new form of idealism, or, perhaps, a
hitherto unprecedented form of insanity.

Like Husserl, Frege regarded *Sinne* as transparent, in that
anyone who grasped the senses of any two expressions must
thereby know whether or not they were the same; and, though
I do not know of any explicit statement to this effect, it seems
reasonable to credit him with the parallel view that no one
could suppose himself to attach a sense to an expression
unless he genuinely did so. If we could also attribute to him
the premiss that for no *Sinn* can it be guaranteed that a
Bedeutung corresponds, the conclusion would follow that we
can never know whether there is anything about which we are
speaking or of which we are thinking. This would yield a type
of intellectual scepticism: acceptance of the sceptic's argument would result in an intellectualised idealism. It would,
once again, be an uneasy variety of idealism, because a *Sinn*
purports to present a referent – to be the manner in which
some referent is given to us: so, although, in merely
entertaining a thought, and not yet judging it to be true or
false, we commit no actual error, still the thought presents
itself to us as being either true or false, and hence as having
referents corresponding to its constituent senses, and, if it
purports to be about an object, as having a genuine object to
be about. Yet, however uneasy such an intellectualised
idealism might be, the premiss would leave Frege's realist
doctrine open to attack from it. If Frege showed no anxiety on

this score, that is because he did not accept the premiss. He believed that natural language contains expressions possessing sense but lacking reference: but he believed also that this is a grave defect of natural language, which requires correction before we have at our disposal a language within which we can reason with an assurance of the validity of our inferences, and hence a language serviceable for scientific purposes. To devise such a language is possible only if there is a way of framing, or of introducing, singular terms so as to confer on them a sense for which there is a guarantee that a reference corresponds: the premiss must therefore be false.

This is not the place to discuss by what means Frege believed that he had guaranteed a reference for the singular terms of the symbolic language of *Grundgesetze* – a belief that was plainly mistaken, in view of the inconsistency of the theory. All that matters is that he believed that he did possess a means to frame singular terms that were not only Russellian in Evans's sense that they would express no sense unless they had a reference, but of which we could *know* that they had a reference; and, further, that, without such a means, he would have been powerless to counter an attack from a form of idealism.

Russell's arguments, in 'On Denoting', against Frege's distinction between sense and reference, or, as he expresses it, between meaning and denotation, are obscure and contorted; they have resisted attempts to elucidate them or render them cogent. It seems probable, however, that they should be understood as an expression, even if somewhat confused, of his primary motive for rejecting the distinction. That motive was to safeguard realism. Russell plainly believed that, once he had distinguished between sense and reference, Frege *was* powerless to counter an attack from idealism. Realism could be secure, he thought, only if, when a sentence was correctly analysed, the meaning of every genuinely significant phrase within it could be taken to consist in its standing for some component of extra-linguistic and extra-mental reality, which would then be a genuine constituent of the proposition the sentence expressed. This plainly could not be done for definite descriptions. They could be taken to be genuinely significant constituents of the sentence only if their meanings were distinguished from their denotations; and then realism would be at risk. That was why the theory of descriptions appeared to Russell a discovery of such fundamental importance. By means of it, a denoting phrase such as a definite description could be declared not to *have* a meaning, "because", as Russell wrote, "in any proposition in which it occurs, the proposition, fully expressed, does not contain the phrase, which has been broken up".[7]

Like Frege's, Husserl's theory was capable of blocking an intellectualised idealism only if objectual reference was in some cases guaranteed. Barry Smith holds that this condition was not satisfied by Husserl's theory of noemata, as expounded in *Ideen*, but that it *was* satisfied by the theory set out in the *Logische Untersuchungen*: for, according to it, "linguistic acts are in every case built up on the basis of the low-grade intentionality of sensory acts, and the latter are guaranteed objectual correlates".[8] The claim seems weak. Sensation is, of course, an essential ingredient of perception, even of delusive perception. Husserl regarded sensation as a dependent part (*Moment*) of the complex perceptual act, of which the other dependent part was an objectivising interpretation (*objektivierende Auffassung*); but he was perfectly well aware that perceptions may be delusive. Sensations being only dependent parts of perceptual acts as a whole, they "are indeed, in naive intuitive presentation, *components* of the presentational experience, ... but in no way its *objects*".[9] As for linguistic acts, Husserl admittedly makes use of a notion of a meaning-fulfilling act, in which we perceive the state of affairs we are stating to obtain; but the act of stating it to obtain has its meaning independently of whether it is, in this sense, fulfilled. If, then, there is some

[7] B. Russell, *Essays in Conceptual Analysis*, ed. D. Lackey, London, 1973, p. 114.
[8] B. Smith, op. cit., p. 170.
[9] *Logische Untersuchungen*, Investigation I, Chap. 2, §23.

sense in which sensation guarantees its objects, a claim in itself dubious, this seems of trifling importance for securing a guarantee that intentional acts will sufficiently often have objectual reference to ward off the threat of idealism. However this may be, Smith is at one with Philipse in considering that Husserl's introduction of noemata, with the accompanying phenomenological reduction, was a step along the long and thorny road to transcendental idealism; and they are surely right.

CHAPTER 9

Frege on Perception

(i) Subjective and objective sense: the example of colour-words

There are only two passages in Frege's writings, widely separated in time, that contain any substantial remarks about sense-perception. The first occurs in *Grundlagen*, §26, where, in the context of the distinction between the subjective and the objective, he discusses the meanings of colour-words. In §24 he had said, "When we see a blue surface, we have a particular impression, which corresponds to the word 'blue'; and we recognise this again, when we observe another blue surface". This seems a very ordinary remark, but it is not his last word on the subject: in §26 he treats the matter as follows:

> In connection with the word "white" we usually think of a certain sensation, which, naturally, is wholly subjective; but it seems to me that even in ordinary linguistic usage an objective sense is frequently prominent. If one calls snow white, one means to express an objective character, which in ordinary daylight we recognise by means of a certain sensation. If the light is coloured, one will take that into account in forming one's judgement. One may perhaps say, "It *appears* red now, but it *is* white". Even a colour-blind person can speak of red and green, although he does not distinguish these colours in sensation. He recognises the distinction by the fact that others make it, or perhaps by means of a physical experiment. The

colour-word thus often designates, not our subjective sensation, of which we cannot know that it agrees with that of
another – for obviously the use of the same name provides no
guarantee – but an objective character.

He thus concludes that what constitutes objectivity is
independence of our sensations, intuitions and ideas.

The thought, the almost irresistible thought, whose truth
Frege never doubted, that none of us can ever know whether
the sensations of others resemble his own, prompts Frege to
make a sharp distinction between subjective and objective
senses of colour-words. He does not, indeed, use the
expression "subjective sense", but merely refers to sensations
as subjective; but the phrase "objective sense" implies the
existence of a subjective one. To this it might well be objected
that, even if sensations are subjective, the sense of the word
"sensation" is objective and communicable: indeed, Frege had
originally distinguished senses in general, as being objective,
from subjective ideas, regardless of whether what they
referred or applied to was itself subjective or objective. Yet a
sense involving essential reference to an item accessible only
to a single subject, such as a sensation, conceived as private as
Frege conceived it, would necessarily be incommunicable.
This shows, not that the thesis that senses are not mental
contents was mistaken, but that the *ground* offered for it,
namely the communicability and hence the objectivity of
senses, was not completely correct: for an incommunicable
sense relating to a private sensation would still not be a
content of the mind like the sensation itself.

Wittgenstein's critique of the private ostensive definition[1]
implies that colour-words can have no such subjective,
incommunicable sense as Frege supposed: but, in any case,
Frege argued that, since we use colour-words to communicate
with one another, they must, when so used, bear a different,
objective sense. In just the same spirit, he was to argue in 'Der
Gedanke' that, when someone uses the word "I" in soliloquy, it
expresses a sense that only he can grasp, namely the way in

[1] *Philosophical Investigations*, I-§§243-311.

which he is given to himself, and in which he cannot be given to anybody else, but that, when he uses it to communicate to others, it must bear a different sense that his hearers can grasp as well as he. Frege's claim concerning the 'objective sense' is now a commonplace: no one would now deny that the application of colour-words, as words of the common language, must be governed by common criteria and hence capable of being decided to the common satisfaction; if the claim appeared at the time less obvious, that was only because philosophers were then prone to think more about interior thought and less about the content of those thoughts we communicate to one another. But an uneasiness remains. Does not Frege's dichotomy between the subjective and objective senses of colour-words do violence to the unity of the meanings we attach to them? Are not those meanings essentially bound up with our colour-vision? Is there really *no* sense in which a colour-blind man cannot fully grasp the meaning of "red"?

Frege's account in this passage is not quite coherent. Objectivity requires independence from sensation. Hence the colour-word, considered as applied, in its objective sense, to opaque objects, is to signify an objective character of their surfaces, one, presumably, that they would have whether we could recognise it or not; a colour-blind man must therefore be able to know what character of surfaces it is that it signifies. But those who are not colour-blind recognise that character from the visual sensation to which it gives rise in them; and even the colour-blind may recognise it from others' so recognising it. The objective sense of the colour-word thus appears not, after all, to have that independence from sensation that Frege holds objectivity to require. Now what is lacking from *Grundlagen* is the distinction between sense and reference. Even while retaining his belief in the radical privacy of sensations, Frege could have improved his account by appeal to this distinction. On such a modified account, the *reference* of a colour-word (as applied to opaque objects) would be an objective property of physical surfaces, and correspondingly when it is applied to transparent objects or to sources of light: but each speaker would attach to it a *sense* relating to his private colour-impression. As an objective feature of physical objects, a colour would, on this account, have no intrinsic connection with our visual sensations, which is why the colour-blind man is able to refer to it; but the *sense* which a normally sighted person attaches to the colour-word is directly connected with his colour vision.

This treatment of the topic is as far as Frege would have been able to go without calling the incommunicability of sensations in question; but it is plainly not satisfactory. When Frege speaks of our saying, of a white object seen in a red light, "It *looks* red", he is not meaning to have each person speak of his private visual impression: it is as much an objective matter that the object looks red in that light as it is that it *is* white. There are two degrees of deviation from the categorical "is": someone comes closer to the categorical statement when he says simply, "It looks red", than when he says, "It looks red to me". But even the latter cannot be construed as a report of a sense-impression private in Frege's radical conception of privacy. It is useless to qualify the incommunicability of such private sensations by saying that we cannot completely convey to others, or convey to them with certainty, what the sensation is like: if the sensation were private in the way Frege believed it to be, we could not convey it to others *at all*; for how would anyone else so much as begin to understand what "red" meant when used as the name of a private sense-impression? There can be no vocabulary for features of sense-experience considered as unadulterated by interpretation of it as perception of external reality; and, as is now very generally agreed, if there could, we could not by means of it give any faithful report of our sense-experience, which is saturated with such interpretations. The only proper explanation of the form of sentence "It looks (sounds, feels, etc.) F to me" is therefore as meaning "I judge from looking at it (listening to it, touching it, etc.) that it is F, or at least should so judge were it not for some extraneous knowledge that I have". When someone looks at one of the drawings producing a standard optical illusion, he judges one line to be longer than the other. Having measured them, he establishes that they have the same length, but the one still *looks* longer to him. This is just to say that, simply by looking, and without adverting to the knowledge that he has acquired by measuring the lines, he would still judge it to be longer.

Such an account of the sense of "looks" makes "is red" prior in the order of explanation to "looks red": but this rules out the most obvious way of explaining the connection between colours and human visual abilities. "Red" does not merely signify a physical property: it signifies an *observable* property; and its doing so is most easily secured if we can explain "It is red" as meaning "It looks red to normally sighted people in normal lighting". If, however, we have explained "looks red" in terms of "is red", we are debarred from also explaining "is red", in turn, in terms of "looks red". How can we escape from this circle?

The modified version of Frege's account was unsatisfactory because, while allowing the word "red" a common reference, it ascribed a distinct sense to "red" in the mouth of each speaker. Our problem is thus to explain the sense, shared by different speakers, which the word has in the common language, and to do so in such a way as to display why it is a grammatical observation, in Wittgenstein's sense, that (in favourable circumstances) we can tell whether something is red by looking at it. Now there are two kinds of case in which we may say that someone tells that an object has a certain characteristic by looking at it. Sherlock Holmes could tell, just by looking at him, that a client did a great deal of writing: he did so by noticing the shininess of his right cuff and the smooth patch on his left elbow. The temptation to assimilate to cases of this type that in which one tells, by looking at it, that an object is red forces us to take the visual impression as playing the role played, in the first case, by the shiny cuffs: one tells that the object is red from the visual sensation. But, in saying this, we go round in a circle: for there is no way of characterising a visual impression as of something red save as a state in which, simply by looking, and prescinding from any collateral information, one would judge that there was something red there. There is no answer to the question by what one judges, from looking at it, that the object is red, save "By its colour", which is to say nothing. In a case of the Sherlock Holmes type, we know what it is for someone to do a great deal of writing even though it has never occurred to us that one could tell that simply by looking at him, and that is why there has to be an informative answer to the question how Holmes can tell that; but someone's claim to know what it was for an object to be red would come into question if it appeared that he was unaware that one could tell that it was red by looking at it. Our problem is to explain the conceptual connection between the objective property of being red and the epistemological character of its being an observational property. This character consists in our ability to tell by looking that an object possesses the property; it is on that, rather than on the notion of something's looking red, that we should fasten our attention.

An inclination may be felt to compare the predicate "is red" with predicates like "is interesting" and "is amusing". The latter predicates have a flimsy objective sense: one can dispute over whether something is really interesting or really amusing. But the objective sense is clearly dependent upon the subjective notion of finding something interesting or amusing; something *is* interesting or amusing if most reasonably intelligent people would find it so. That is undoubtedly correct: the concepts of being interesting and of being amusing could not be explained save by reference to human reactions. The presumed analogue is of course that we should explain what it is for something to be red as its looking red, in normal light, to most people with normal vision: the concept of being red could thus be explained only by reference to human visual sensations. There is, however, no true parallelism between the concepts 'interesting' and 'amusing' and colour-concepts. For one thing, the former have only a single grade of subjectivity: to the statement, "It is not interesting", one may reply, "*I* find it interesting", but not, "It seems interesting even if it is not". But the second difference rather intensifies the difficulty concerning the concept 'red'.

There is no danger of circularity in characterising the quasi-objective sense of "interesting" in terms of the subjective notion, since, for someone to find something interesting, it is not necessary that he have the concept 'interesting': to be interested in something is to have a certain reaction or to display a certain attitude towards it, which one can have or display without being able to classify it. But something can look red to someone only if he has the concept 'red': and the only manifestation of its doing so is that he *says* that it is or looks red. It is only those who have received a certain training in the use of colour-words who can manifest their colour-impressions; and it is only to them that we can confidently ascribe colour-impressions.

Philosophers seldom notice the restricted application of colour-words as these are first taught to children. They first learn to recognise bright primary colours, together with white and black, as shown in a book. The uses of the colour-words are presented to them as right or wrong, but no place is yet supplied for such expressions as "looks red": they are simply trained to give the *correct* answers. At this stage, they have an immense amount still to learn before they have acquired the colour-concepts possessed by adults. They do not know how to apply colour-words to transparent substances or to light-sources, and, when they first extend the application of the words to these things, they will make mistakes, such as calling water 'white'. Largely for this reason, they cannot yet appreciate the special place of 'white' and 'black' among colour-concepts: they do not know, for example, that only a white surface will appear red when seen through a red transparent medium, blue when seen through a blue transparent medium, etc., and that only a black surface will appear the same whatever medium it is seen through. They have as yet no conception of differences in appearance due to the distance from which something is seen – how an apparently uniformly coloured surface may resolve into differently coloured dots when inspected closely, or how distant objects take on a blue tinge. They have so far been taught to apply colour-words only to matt surfaces, and cannot allow for the gleams that characterise glossy ones, nor be aware of the change in the appearance of a reflecting surface such as that of water in a pond or coffee in a cup according to the depth of focus of the eyes. They have not yet appreciated how many intermediate and indeterminate shades are to be seen, nor learned to make allowance for the great variation in the appearance at any time of a uniformly coloured surface such as a ceiling or a wall, owing to shadows and reflections from other nearby surfaces, let alone for its variation over time in different types of 'normal' lighting.

A child who has mastered the first stage in learning the use of colour-words thus has a great deal more to learn before he has attained to the adult use: but, still, what he has learned is an indispensable foundation for the rest, and it is therefore profitable to ask in what his grasp of the senses of colour-words, at that stage, consists. For the reasons already given, we have to resist the temptation to reply that he associates each colour-word with a particular type of visual impression, and that it is by means of that visual impression that he is able to name correctly the colours in the book. He does not recognise the colours *by* anything: he simply recognises them. For him, the colours of things in his picture-book are objective in the sense that there is right or wrong in naming them, and agreement about them, at least by adults: he has no conception of any independent basis on which he assigns the colours, colour-impressions about which he might be right even if they had misled him about the objective colours. His grasp of the senses of the colour-words consists solely in the recognitional capacity he has acquired: he conceives of the colours simply as features he is capable of recognising by looking.

It is on this primitive capacity for recognising colours that our mature understanding of colour-words is based. As children, we have acquired a propensity to apply colour-names to surfaces of bright uniform hue. In learning to extend this propensity so as to apply them to opaque surfaces in general, as well as to light-sources and transparent substances, our practice becomes ever more complex and subtle. We learn to make automatic allowance for lighting effects, shadows and reflections, and, in doing so, our readiness to judge that a surface is white or red is modified in complex ways. It would now no longer be misleading to say that we have come to consider colours as dispositional properties, in that we take it as part of what constitutes a surface's being red that it takes on an orange tinge in the vicinity of a yellow surface or a purple one when seen in a blue light or through a blue medium. Only an unusual effect, such as occurs in certain optical illusions involving colours, or with certain unfamiliar lighting, will generate a gap between the colour that a surface has and that which it appears to have, since, while we may know in advance of this effect, we allow for it only by consciously invoking our knowledge, which thus remains extraneous. In such exceptional cases, the sense of saying, "It looks red", is correctly captured by the formula, "Were it not for our extraneous knowledge, we should, by looking at it, judge it to be red". But the variety of factors for which we have learned to make unreflective allowance enables us, with a certain effort, to prescind from those factors, and so to employ a more refined sense of "looks red", to be glossed as "If we were unaware of the lighting (the reflections, the shadows), we should judge it to be red". Here we approach the kind of scrutiny to which a surface must be subjected by a painter who wishes to recreate the visual impression; there are not, however, two sharply distinguished senses of "looks", but, rather, a gradation, according to how many of the factors we should normally take into account in judging the colour we choose to prescind from. These more refined notions of looking red, etc., are what make possible a dispositional conception of colours; if we were not consciously aware of the factors for which we make allowance in judging the colours of objects, and hence unable to prescind from them in thought, colours would remain purely categorical features for us, as they are for children in the first stage of mastering colour vocabulary. Philosophers usually understand a dispositional analysis of colours to be expressed by the phenomenalist formula, "An object is red if it looks red to normally sighted viewers in a normal light", and this is far too crude: it is an integral part of being red to look orange in some circumstances and purple in others, in a suitably refined sense of "look". More to the point, our concept of looking red rests on our capacity to recognise surfaces as being red by looking at them, a capacity which, in rudimentary form, we acquire at the first stage of learning colour-words. The concept of looking red thus remains dependent on that of being red, not conversely: colours are observational properties, not because we identify them by means of reidentifiable sense-data, but because our colour concepts rest ultimately upon an ability, acquired by training, to recognise colours by observation.

By speaking, in *Grundlagen*, of the senses of colour-words as 'objective', Frege intended to say that these words are understood as denoting objective properties of physical surfaces. Was he right to do so? His failure to allow a category intermediate between the radically subjective and the totally objective makes the question difficult to answer. A property is objective in the weak sense if the possession of that property by an object is independent of any one individual's sensations or other reactions; it is objective in the strong sense if its possession is independent of all human sensations and reactions whatever. Now a child at the first stage of learning about colours certainly conceives of them as objective properties of certain physical surfaces in the weak sense of "objective"; and the same applies to the adult, who has developed a more sophisticated capacity for recognising colours by taking physical circumstances into account of which the child has no knowledge. The senses attached to colour-words, by both child and adult, if they have normal sight, are given by their respective recognitional capacities; it is thus intrinsic to these senses that the colour-words are taken to denote observational properties. There is no reason to regard different individuals as attaching different senses to the same colour-word, since it is integral to those senses that the relevant recognitional capacity is understood, by both child and adult, as shared with all other normally sighted people. The blind and the colour-blind, on the other hand, may also regard colours as observational properties, conceiving of them as properties that others can recognise by sight; but they cannot attach the same senses to colour-words as the normally sighted, because they lack the capacity to recognise what they apply to. The distinction between the senses and the references of colour-words, or between our concepts of the various colours and the colours themselves, considered as properties of physical surfaces, is therefore still required.

The most important difference between the child's concept of colours and the adult's is that the child has no conception of objectivity in the strong sense, whereas the adult does. The concept of a colour as an objective property in the weak sense in no way guarantees that it may be regarded as objective in the stronger sense: it might be like the property of being interesting, which is unlikely to be explicable without reference to human reactions. It is not intrinsic to the concept of taste, for example, that there be any means of determining whether or not a given substance is sweet other than the reactions of men and beasts who take it into their mouths. Since we have to admit a distinction between the sense and the reference of the words "sweet" and "red", however, the possibility was open from the start that we should find a way of identifying the property without reference to human recognitional capacities. As adults, we have a strong drive to discover what physical properties are in themselves; that is, to find a means of characterising them independently of the limitations of human perceptual powers and of the particular point of view of creatures of a certain size and occupying a certain region of space at a certain epoch. This we can, of course, do for colours; a surface is red if it tends to reflect light of longer wave-length and to absorb that of shorter. Objectivity in the strong sense should not, indeed, be confused with real existence: even if tastes were not objective in this sense, a metaphysical denial that sugar is really sweet would be quite unwarranted. Philosophers who deny that there are any colours in external reality commit a double mistake: they confuse strong objectivity with reality, and they fail to distinguish sense from reference. But the salient fact is that we cannot dispense with a distinction between the strong sense of "objective" and the weak sense, for which the term "intersubjective" may be used instead. It is a marked deficiency of Frege's discussion of objectivity that he never admits such a distinction; and the defect is especially apparent in his brief discussion of the senses of colour-words.

(ii) Sensation and thought

The second passage in which Frege discusses sense-perception comes from an essay, 'Der Gedanke', published thirty years later. In it, he stresses the part played by conceptual thought in our perceptions of physical reality: though he still insists on the privacy of sense-impressions, the notion plays a less dubious role than in his earlier discussion. Using the term "thing", which I accordingly write with an initial capital, to mean a material object, he writes as follows:

Sense-impressions on their own do not disclose the external world to us. There are, perhaps, beings who only have sense-impressions, without seeing or feeling Things. To have visual impressions is not yet to see Things. How does it come about that I see the tree in just that place where I see it? It obviously depends on the visual impressions that I have, and on the particular kind of visual impressions that arise because I see with two eyes. On each of my two retinas there is formed a particular image, in the physical sense. Someone else sees the tree in the same place. He, too, has two retinal images, which, however, differ from mine. We must assume that these retinal images determine our impressions. We thus have visual impressions that are not only not identical, but markedly divergent from one another. And yet we move about in the same external world. Having visual impressions is, indeed, necessary for seeing Things, but it is not sufficient. What has still to be added is not anything sensible. And yet it is precisely this which opens up the external world for us; for without this non-sensible component each person would remain shut up within his own inner world ... Besides one's inner world, one must distinguish the external world proper of sensible, perceptible Things and also the realm of that which is not sensorily perceptible. To recognise either of these two realms we stand in need of something non-sensible; but in the sensory perception of Things we have need, in addition, of sense-impressions, and these belong wholly to the inner world.[2]

Frege is here distinguishing between three realms of existence of which each of us is conscious: the inner world, which comprises the contents of his consciousness and is private to him; the external world of material objects, which we all inhabit together; and the 'third realm' of thoughts and their constituent senses, which is likewise accessible to all in common, but whose contents are immutable and immaterial, and do not act on the senses or on each other, but which we can grasp.

> We do not *have* a thought, in the way that we have a sense-impression, say; but we also do not *see* a thought, as we see, say, a star. It is therefore advisable to choose a special expression, and for this purpose the verb "to grasp" suggests itself.[3]

At an earlier stage, Frege had, of course, recognised a great variety of objects that, unlike the contents of consciousness, are objective, but, unlike material objects, are not 'actual', that is to say, do not have causal effects; among these were logical objects such as numbers. But I think that, at the time of writing 'Der Gedanke', he had ceased to believe in logical objects: so thoughts and their constituent senses could be taken to exhaust the population of the third realm. The passage which I quoted at length is tantalisingly incomplete, one of the reasons being that Frege was not intending to set out a theory of perception, but simply to argue that we must have access to the 'third realm'. Plainly, the non-sensible component of perception, which converts it from a mere sense-impression, belonging to the inner world, into the

[2] 'Der Gedanke', p. 75.
[3] Ibid., p. 74.

perception of a material object, and so opens up the external world to us, belongs to the 'third realm'. But it is left unstated whether it must be a complete thought, for instance to the effect that there is a tree in a certain place, or whether it may be a mere thought-constituent, for instance the sense of the concept-word "tree", involving our seeing the object *as* a tree. It is also left unstated whether, if it is a whole thought, the act of perception involves *judging* that the thought is true, or whether it is sufficient merely to grasp the thought without advancing from it to the truth-value.

Almost certainly, Frege meant that a whole thought is involved, and that, in normal cases, the perceiver will judge this thought to be true. The context principle, as stated in *Grundlagen*, namely that a word has meaning only in the context of a sentence, suggests that Frege held a strong thesis concerning understanding, which I will call the *dependence thesis*: viz, that it is possible to grasp the sense of a word only as it occurs in some particular sentence, and hence possible to grasp a constituent of a thought, not itself amounting to a whole thought, only *as* a constituent of that or some other thought. Even if it will bear this interpretation, however, it would be dangerous to appeal to the context principle as a guide to Frege's abiding views, since he never reaffirmed it in that form after *Grundlagen*: moreover, the echo of it that occurs in *Grundgesetze* is a principle governing *reference*, and not sense.[4] It would nevertheless be plausible to attribute to him a restriction of the dependence thesis to the senses of

---

[4] *Grundgesetze*, Vol. I, §§10 and 29. In §32 Frege characterises the thought expressed by a sentence as the thought that the conditions for it to be true are fulfilled, and the sense of a constituent of a sentence as its contribution to the expression of that thought. This latter specification can be seen as what the context principle becomes when interpreted as a principle governing *sense*. On its own, it might be thought to sustain the dependence thesis; but Frege should surely be taken as meaning that the sense is the contribution to the thought expressed by *every* sentence in which the expression occurs. Even that will not exclude the dependence thesis; but that thesis is excluded, for 'saturated' expressions (those containing no argument-place), if we take the sense as consisting in the way in which the referent is determined, which *is* the contribution it makes to the determination of the truth or falsity of the whole.

incomplete or unsaturated expressions like predicates, since their senses, as well as their referents, are said themselves to be unsaturated, and hence, presumably, incapable of standing on their own. If this is correct, the grasp of the sense of a concept-word could not be an ingredient of perception save as an inextricable constituent of the grasp of a whole thought. As for whether perception involves judgement, or only the apprehension of a thought without judging it to be true, that depends on whether perception yields knowledge or not, since Frege explicitly (and unsurprisingly) held that knowledge issues in judgements;[5] since he also accepted sense-perception as a source of knowledge, the natural conclusion is that, at least in the normal case, perception involves judging some state of affairs to obtain, rather than merely entertaining the thought that it does.

We can make little further headway with Frege's views on perception, as stated in 'Der Gedanke', until we have a better understanding of his notion of grasping a thought or a thought-constituent (a sense): to this we must therefore now turn.

---

[5] 'Logik' (1897), *Posthumous Writings*, p. 144.

CHAPTER 10

Grasping a Thought

The notion that Frege so persistently employs, that of grasping a sense or a thought, requires close scrutiny. Two distinctions naturally suggest themselves. Sometimes the phrase "grasping the sense of a sentence" or "of a word" is equivalent to "understanding the sentence" (or "the word"): to grasp the sense of the sentence is to recognise the sentence as having that sense. In other cases, someone may be said to grasp the sense of an expression even if he does not understand the expression (because, say, he does not know the language to which it belongs), provided that he has the concept which it expresses (in the non-Fregean sense of "concept"); likewise he may be said to grasp the thought expressed by a sentence, and hence its sense, even though he does not understand that sentence. We might call these the *intensional* and *extensional* interpretations of the phrase "to grasp the sense of the sentence" (or "of the expression").

How far is the extensional interpretation needed? A case in which we appear to need it arises in discussion of Frege's criterion for sameness of sense. He sometimes expresses the condition for two sentences A and B to express the same thought as being that anyone who grasps the thought expressed by A and that expressed by B, and recognises either as true, must unhesitatingly recognise the other as true.[1] As it stands, however, this criterion is implausible, as can be

---

[1] See, for example, *Funktion und Begriff*, p. 14, and 'Kurze Übersicht meiner logischen Lehren' (1906), *Posthumous Writings*, p. 197.

seen from the example concerning directions used in
Grundlagen, §§ 64-8. If we take A as "Line a is parallel to line
b", and B as "The direction of line a is the same as that of line
b", the criterion is satisfied, and Frege indeed says, in
Grundlagen §64, that, in passing from A to B, "we split up the
content in a way different from the original one", implying
that both sentences express the same judgeable content (the
same thought, in his later terminology). This is, however,
counter-intuitive. To grasp the thought expressed by B (even
on the extensional interpretation of this phrase), one must
have the concept of a direction, whereas one need have no
grasp of this concept in order to grasp the thought expressed
by A. Indeed, Frege admits as much, claiming that, by
splitting up the content in a different way, "we thereby attain
a new concept". In a similar way, he claims in *Funktion und
Begriff* that the statements "For every x, $x^2 - 4x = x(x - 4)$"
and "The value-range of the function $x^2 - 4x$ is the same as
that of the function $x(x - 4)$" both "express the same sense, but
in a different way",[2] a claim to which there is a precisely
analogous objection. This instance is, of course, a special case
of Axiom V of *Grundgesetze*, which generated Russell's
contradiction within Frege's system: if Frege's claim were
correct, however, there could be nothing amiss with that
axiom.

In *Grundgesetze* itself, Frege did not attempt to maintain
that the two sides of Axiom V – that stating that, for every
argument, the functions have the same values and that
stating that they have the same value-ranges – expressed the
same thought; and this was wise of him. For it is impossible to
frame a coherent conception of the content of a sentence, or of
a thought that may be expressed by a sentence, according to
which whether or not it is necessary to grasp a given concept
in order to understand the sentence depends only upon how
the sentence is framed, and not upon its content or on the
thought that it expresses. To grasp the thought that planets
have elliptical orbits, for example, it is necessary to have the

[2] *Funktion und Begriff*, p. 11.

concept of an ellipse: it would be incomprehensible were anyone to deny this on the ground that it depended merely on how that thought was expressed. This consideration therefore prompts the following emendation of Frege's criterion for the identity of thoughts: the sentences A and B express the same thought if anyone who grasps the thought expressed by either thereby grasps that expressed by the other, and, if he recognises either as true, must unhesitatingly recognise the other as true. Here it is of course not meant that whoever understands either sentence must understand the other, since he might happen not to know some of the words occurring in it: it is meant that he must grasp the thought, which he might express in some other way, that is in fact expressed by that sentence. It is therefore essential in this context to understand the phrase "to grasp the thought" according to its extensional interpretation.

A further distinction, to which Frege himself never adverts, is the familiar one between a dispositional and an occurrent grasp of a sense or thought. Consider the passage with which the essay 'Gedankengefüge' of 1923 opens:

> It is astonishing what language can do, in that, with a few syllables, it can express unsurveyably many thoughts, so that it can find a clothing even for a thought that has been grasped by an inhabitant of the Earth for the very first time, in which it will be understood by someone else to whom it is entirely new. This would not be possible if we could not distinguish parts in the thought corresponding to the parts of a sentence, so that the structure of the sentence can serve as a picture of the structure of the thought.

Here our capacity to understand a sentence expressing a thought that is entirely new to us is being explained in terms of our existing grasp of the senses of the constituent parts of that sentence; and this grasp is, surely, a dispositional one. When, on the other hand, Frege speaks of the very first time that an inhabitant of the Earth grasps a given thought, he is, presumably, speaking of grasping a thought in an occurrent sense. The individual has surely long had the *capacity* to frame such a thought, as has the person to whom he communicates it: it is just that this is the first time he, or any other human being, has expressly entertained that thought.

It seems natural to say that, in considering complete thoughts, the occurrent notion of grasping a thought is primary, whereas, when we consider single words, the dispositional notion of grasping their sense is primary. What interests us, concerning single words, is whether a subject will understand them when he hears them, or is able to use them when he has occasion to, not whether he has their senses in mind at a particular moment, save when he hears or uses a sentence containing them. Likewise, we are more interested in whether someone does or does not have a given concept (in the non-Fregean sense of "concept") than in whether he is currently exercising his grasp of it. By contrast, what is important about a sentence is not whether he is capable of understanding it, but whether he understands it on a particular occasion on which he hears it. Likewise, what is important about a thought is not whether he is capable of grasping it, or even whether he is familiar with it, but whether he is currently apprehending it – having that thought, considering it, judging it to be true or regarding it as having been asserted.

Now grasping a sense, dispositionally understood, is plainly not a mental act, but a kind of ability. It is on this ground that Wittgenstein argues that understanding is not a mental process; in so arguing, he expressly compares it to an ability.[3] When, by contrast, Frege acknowledges that, although thoughts are not mental contents, grasping a thought is a mental act – one directed towards something external to the mind[4] – he must be construing the notion of grasping a thought in its occurrent sense. Wittgenstein labours to dispel the supposition that there is any occurrent sense of "understand". If this could be successfully maintained, the conception of understanding an utterance could be reduced to that of hearing it, while possessing a dispositional under-

---

[3] *Philosophical Investigations*, I-§§150, 153-4, and p. 59, below the line.
[4] 'Logik' (1897), *Posthumous Writings*, p. 145.

standing of the words it contains and the constructions it
employs. But it is difficult to see how it can be maintained
that no occurrent notion of understanding is required: for it is
possible to be perplexed by a sentence on first hearing,
through a failure to take in its structure, and to attain an
understanding of it on reflection.

All this still leaves us in perplexity about what exactly *is* a
grasp of a sense, or of a thought, as Frege uses these notions.
For him, the sense itself is the logical notion: when we are
concerned to characterise the sense of an expression or of a
sentence, we should pay no attention to the process of
grasping that sense, which is an irrelevant psychological
matter.[5] He therefore seldom devotes any attention to the
process. One of the few exceptions occurs in the lecture-course
'Logik in der Mathematik' of 1914. Frege has been advocating
the Russellian view that definitions are mere abbreviations,
and hence logically unimportant (a view in conflict with that
expressed in *Grundlagen* concerning the scientific fruit-
fulness of definitions). He now says, in a passage partly
quoted in Chapter 7:

> Logical unimportance is by no means the same as psychologi-
> cal unimportance. When we consider intellectual work as it
> actually proceeds, we find that a thought is by no means
> always present to our consciousness clearly in all its parts.
> When we use the word "integral", for example, are we always
> conscious of everything that belongs to the sense of this word?
> Only in very rare cases, I think. Usually just the word is
> present to our consciousness, though associated with a more or
> less dim knowledge that this word is a sign that has a sense,
> and that, when we wish, we can recall this sense. But the
> consciousness that we can do this usually satisfies us. If we
> tried to recall everything belonging to the sense of this word,
> we should make no headway. Our consciousness is simply not
> sufficiently comprehensive. We often have need of a sign with
> which we associate a very complex sense. This sign serves us as
> a receptacle in which we can, as it were, carry the sense about,
> in the consciousness that we can always open this receptacle

[5] Ibid.

should we have need of what it contains.[6]

At this point Frege goes on actually to use these reflections to reinforce his distinction between the logical and the psychological:

> From this consideration it is apparent that the thought, as I understand the word, in no way coincides with a content of my consciousness.

The view thus expressed differs strongly from the Humpty-Dumpty view advocated by Husserl, that a word or expression is invested with meaning by a mental act on the speaker's part conferring meaning upon it. For Frege a word simply *has* a sense: its bearing that sense in the mouth of a speaker does not depend upon his performing any mental act of endowing it with that sense. On the contrary, even in thinking to himself, he may use the word without adverting to its sense, confident only that he can call the sense to mind when he needs to. When *will* he need to, then? Evidently, when it is necessary to do so in order to judge that a sentence containing the word is true, or that it is false, or to decide what follows deductively from that sentence or whether it follows from certain others. His grasp of the sense is therefore, we may say, an ability which is called into play in determining the truth-value of the sentence, or in attending to particular features of the manner in which its truth-value may be determined: the speaker or soliloquist employs the word in the confidence that he can recall the contribution the word makes to the truth-conditions of the sentence when it becomes necessary to attend to it.

This is a sympathetic interpretation; and it appears in general accord with Frege's explanations of what the sense of a word consists in. Nevertheless, it is by no means certain that he would have accepted it. Frege had two modes of writing about sense: one when he was concerned with the relation between sense and reference; and one when he was

[6] 'Logik in der Mathematik', *Posthumous Writings*, p. 209.

striving to elaborate the ontological status of senses, involving the mythology of the third realm. The foregoing interpretation of a grasp of sense as an ability fits very well all that he wrote in the former mode; but it plainly does not fit the conception of senses as non-actual but objective and immutable *objects*. In the latter mode, he thought of the sense of a word or of a sentence as something that we apprehend by an exercise of an intellectual faculty somewhat analogous to sense-perception: so, although a sense or thought is not a content of consciousness, it may be an object of conscious attention. This conception makes awareness of a sense highly disanalogous with awareness of a material object, as Frege construed the latter. On the one hand, there is surely nothing corresponding to the sense-impression which forms an integral part of the perception of a physical object: my awareness of the thought, which is *not* a content of my consciousness, is not mediated by some impression of that thought, an impression which *is* a content of consciousness. On the other hand, no *further* sense or thought plays the role which, in sense-perception, Frege thinks is played by something from the third realm. In the latter case, the sense-impression must be accompanied or informed either by the sense of some means of referring to or picking out the object, or by the thought that such an object is present. When we actually refer to a thought or sense, for instance, as the principle of double effect or the second law of thermodynamics, we do so by means of a further sense – that of the term "the principle of double effect", for example – whose referent is the first thought or sense: but grasping a sense is something quite different from referring to it or thinking of it. Grasping a sense is immediate. An object cannot be given to us save in a particular way, the particular way in which it is given constituting a sense to which that object corresponds as referent. But there cannot be different ways in which one and the same sense can be given, since everything that goes to determine the referent is part of the sense. The sense may be *expressed* in different words, in different languages or in the same language: but it is not *given* to us at all, but simply grasped. The third realm is thus far more directly accessible to us than the external world of physical objects. For all that, the human mind is not capacious enough to be able to attend simultaneously to too many senses, or to all the details of any very complex one. The instrument of language nevertheless enables it to handle complicated thoughts, since we can attend to the *words* without, at each moment, attending to all their senses.

This conception is obviously very unsatisfactory. For one thing, it leaves unexplained the manner in which the word acts as a receptacle for the sense: when we reach a point at which we do need to advert to the sense of the word, how do we succeed in calling to mind the right sense? The natural answer is that we have in some manner established an association between the word and its sense, so that the latter comes, as it were, when it is called. The character of such an association is, in the context of Frege's mythology of the third realm, exceedingly mysterious. Moreover, the account fits the case of using an utterly familiar word – "arrive" or "lamp", for example – extremely badly. Someone who uses such a word will be perplexed to say whether, when he uses it, he is attending to its sense: there is for him no such thing as making an effort to recall that sense, and he cannot hear or use the word as if it were one he did not know, any more than someone literate in a given language can see a word written in the script of that language as one ignorant of that script would do.

Frege's account does of course correspond to a common experience, familiar to anyone who has devised or followed a mathematical proof: a term recently introduced by definition, perhaps just for the purpose of the proof, may be used for several steps without appeal to its definition, which is then invoked and which it requires a definite effort to recall. But the mythology of the third realm gets in the way of a clear account. As already remarked, Frege's positive theory of what the sense of an expression consists in is independent of this mythology: it consists in the manner in which its referent is determined, as a step in the determination of the truth-value of any sentence in which the expression occurs. To this, he thinks, the precise mental processes that consciously take place in one who uses the expression, having a dispositional grasp of its sense, are irrelevant: that is why the psychological has to be distinguished from the logical.

What Frege counts as psychological cannot so easily be dismissed from consideration, however. We need to know what exactly it is to grasp a sense, because sense is distinguished from reference precisely by the fact that it can be grasped – can be apprehended directly, rather than in one or another particular way: were it not so, there would be no place for a notion of sense, as distinct from reference, at all. It is, doubtless, because Frege is not disposed to explain a grasp of sense as an ability that he pays no attention to the dispositional/occurrent distinction in connection with it. And what blocks him from giving an account of it as an ability is a fundamental feature of his philosophy: his realism. In order to interpret sense realistically, we must link it, not with *our* procedures for deciding the truth-values of sentences, but with their determination as true or as false by the way things objectively are, independently of our knowledge: by reality itself, as it were. Our grasp of sense consists, therefore, not in the ability to determine the truth-values of sentences, or to recognise them as having one or other truth-value, but in the *knowledge* of what renders them true or false.

We thus cannot, after all, extract from Frege a clear account of what it is to grasp a sense; and we need to know this, in particular, in order to assess the thesis that sense-perception involves the grasp of a thought or sense. Linguistic expressions have a meaning, and it is by no means completely evident that, in explaining in what that meaning consists, we need to explain what it is to know that meaning or to bear it in mind. But it is only a *theory* that anything resembling meaning plays a role in the perception of a physical object: to support that theory, it has to be argued that a grasp of meaning is an ingredient in the (psychological) process of perceiving.

The sympathetic interpretation of a grasp of sense as an ability makes the grasp of sense the primary concept: we now have no account of what a sense is save that embedded in the account of a grasp of that sense. Sense, in other words, has become just the cognate accusative of the verb "to understand". As I have remarked, this does not accord with the mythology, according to which a sense is an independently existing object with which the mind somehow makes contact. But it would have been a further obstacle to Frege's acceptance of the account of a grasp of sense as an ability that it conflicts with his conception of senses as essentially capable of being, but not essentially being, the senses *of* linguistic expressions, that is, with his conception of the relative priority of thought over language. The difficulty does not arise simply from consideration of the notion of grasping a sense. It is, rather, intrinsic to Frege's various doctrines concerning sense itself: on it turns the question whether his two modes of discussing sense can be reconciled. To know that a certain sense is attached to a given word is, on the sympathetic account, to grasp how its presence in a sentence contributes to what is needed to determine the sentence as true or as false. We may readily allow that someone who understands another word, in the same or another language, as making the same contribution attaches the same sense to it: but what would it be to grasp that sense, but not *as* the sense of any actual or even hypothetical word? *We* cannot do that, according to Frege: but we ought to be able to explain what it would be to do it. For his official view is that it is not intrinsic to thoughts to be expressed in language, and that there is no contradiction in supposing beings who can grasp them in their nakedness, divested of linguistic clothing, but that "it is necessary for us men that a thought of which we are conscious is connected in our consciousness with one or another sentence".[7]

The example given earlier, of a natural revision of Frege's criterion for sameness of sense, apparently shows that we cannot quite dispense with a dispositional conception of the grasp of a thought. Equally, we cannot quite dispense with an occurrent conception of the grasp of the sense of a word: for

---

[7] 'Erkenntnisquellen' (1924-5), Section B, *Posthumous Writings*, p. 269.

you may be quite familiar with the fact that a particular word has two distinct senses, and yet, when someone utters a sentence containing it, take it (perhaps wrongly) in just one of those senses. Nevertheless, in the case of a complete thought, the occurrent notion is so much the more salient, and, in that of the sense of a word, the dispositional notion is so much the more salient, that the dependence thesis seems to be generated by a neglect of the occurrent/dispositional distinction. Dispositionally construed, grasping the sense of a word – whether this comprises being aware that the word has that sense, or merely grasping the concept that it in fact expresses, without necessarily understanding the word – does not have a context. The sense of the word may provide for its occurrence in certain contexts and not in others: but the word itself is understood in isolation, in that, if you understand it at all, you thereby grasp its contribution to determining the sense of any larger context in which it can intelligibly occur. Likewise, if someone dispositionally grasps its sense, he thereby understands it as a common component of a great range of complete thoughts, but cannot be said to grasp it only as a component of any one particular thought: you cannot grasp a thought without apprehending it as articulated into components which could occur as parts of other thoughts, and, if you could, you could not be said at all to grasp its components as distinguishable within it. Nevertheless, the dependence thesis cannot so easily be rendered nugatory. A disposition must be capable of being actuated or realised. The dependence thesis may therefore be restated thus: the dispositional grasp of a sense can be activated only in the occurrent grasp of a thought of which that sense is a constituent. That thesis may be plausibly attributed to Frege – at least to the Frege who enunciated the context principle: and it supplies a further ground for holding that that appeal to sense which is involved in sense-perception must consist in the grasp of a complete thought.

CHAPTER 11

Husserl on Perception:
the Generalisation of Meaning

What can be Frege's ground for holding that sense-perception involves the grasp of a sense? It is, presumably, that sense-perception normally requires the awareness of one or more objects, and that we cannot ever simply be aware of an object, in the sense that our state of awareness can be completely described by indicating the object of which we are aware: that object must be given to us in some particular way, and the way in which it is given is always a sense which can be a thought-constituent. The sense-impression may be *of* the object, in the sense that the object gave rise to it, but, being a mere content of consciousness, does not of itself have the capacity to point beyond itself to that object: only a sense – a thought-constituent – has such a capacity to point to something as its referent.

The theory surely has great plausibility: but it suffers from fitting rather badly with Frege's conception of the relation between thought and language. We noted earlier that to conceive of a grasp of sense as an ability conflicts with his view that there is no intrinsic impossibility in grasping a thought in its nakedness, rather than as expressed in words: but his account of perception jars, conversely, with his further view that human beings can grasp only those thoughts which they conceive as the senses of sentences. There are, of course, weaker and stronger interpretations of this requirement. The strongest would be that we can think only in language; the weakest that none of us can have a thought which he is incapable of expressing. Certainly the thesis that sense-perception involves the grasping of a thought or the making of a judgement wars powerfully with a strong interpretation, for it is far from plausible that any remotely conscious linguistic operation is necessary for, or even often accompanies, sensory perception.

In the *Logische Untersuchungen*, Husserl expressed a wholly contrary view of perception.[1] He argued as follows:

> Let us consider an example. I look out into the garden, and give expression to my perception in the words, "A blackbird is flying over!". *What is here the act in which the meaning lies?* ... We should say: it is not the perception, at least not it alone. It is apparent that we cannot describe this situation by saying that, besides the sound of the words, nothing else than the perception is given as determining the significance of the utterance. For an assertion made *on the basis of this same perception* could run quite differently and thereby display a quite *different sense* ... And, conversely, the wording of the sentence, and its *sense*, might remain *the same, while the perception varied in manifold ways.* Every chance alteration in the relative position of the percipient alters the perception itself ...; but such differences are irrelevant to the meaning of the perceptual statement.

He concludes that:

> We cannot suppose that the perception is the act in which the sense of the perceptual statement ... is achieved ...; we shall have to favour, instead, a conception according to which this function of meaning is ascribed to an act of a uniform kind, which is free of the limitations of perception or even of the imagination ...

He allows, however, that it is not merely that the perception prompts the utterance and the act which gives it meaning: rather, when the utterance may be said genuinely to 'express'

[1] Investigation VI, §4.

the perception, the act which gives it meaning is, in a sense which he does not clearly explain, 'united' with the perception.

It is true that, elsewhere in the same book, he faintly adumbrated his later theory. He there said:[2]

> If we imagine a consciousness prior to all experiences, it is a possibility that it has the same *sensations* as we do. But it will see no things and no events involving things, it will perceive no trees or houses, no flight of birds or barking of dogs. Here one immediately feels oneself tempted to express the matter thus: To such a consciousness the sensations do not *mean* anything, they do not *count* for it as *signs* for the properties of an object, nor the complex they form as a sign for the object itself; they are simply lived through, but lack ... an objectifying *interpretation* ... Here, then, we may speak of meaning and of signs just as we do in connection with linguistic and symbolic expressions ... This way of talking ... ought not to be misunderstood as meaning that the consciousness regards the sensations, making them the *objects* of perception, and then adopts an interpretation based upon them ...

Rather, he says, in a phrase already quoted, that in the ordinary case the sensations are "*components* of the perceptual experience – parts of its descriptive content – not at all its *objects*". The upshot is that the perception is constituted by "the experienced complex of sensations being animated by a certain act-character, a certain conception, a certain intention".

In *Ideen*, Husserl introduced his notion of noema, and developed a new account of sense-perception as informed by a noema. This account is not to be equated with Frege's, since, as previously observed, he expressly characterises the notion of noema as a *generalisation* of that of sense or meaning: for instance, in the posthumously published Volume III of *Ideen*, he says quite overtly, "The noema is nothing but a generalisation of the idea of meaning to the entire domain of acts".[3] That immediately rules it out that Husserl could

[2] Investigation I, §23.
[3] *Ideen*, Vol. III, Chap. III, §16; *Husserliana*, Vol. V, ed. M. Biemel, the Hague, 1952, p. 89.

consistently adopt the same explanation of his notion of meaning as Frege gave of his notion of sense. For Frege, a sense is intrinsically a constituent of thoughts, and, as he remarks in a sentence from 'Der Gedanke' already quoted, "thoughts stand in the closest connection with truth".[4] A sense is for him an instruction, as it were, for a step in the determination of a thought as true or false; the step consists in determining a referent of the appropriate logical type, and the instruction a particular means for doing so. (In view of Frege's realism, the instruction must be thought of as addressed, not to us, but to reality.) Thoughts, as Frege conceived of them, are unlike anything else in that they alone are capable of being characterised as true or as false, and their constituents are therefore likewise unlike anything else. Whatever serves the purpose of a sense – whatever constitutes a particular means of determining an object or a function – *is* a sense, forming part of various thoughts; whatever does not serve that purpose cannot in the least resemble a sense. Quite a different conception of sense or meaning is required if we are to have anything that can be generalised, as Husserl wished to generalise it to obtain the notion of noema.

To this it might be objected that Husserl's generalisation consists solely in detaching the sense from any linguistic means of expressing it. This interpretation appears to accord with some of his explanations. For instance, he says in *Ideen*:[5]

> These words ["mean" and "meaning"] relate in the first instance only to the linguistic sphere, to that of "expressing". It is, however, almost inevitable, and, at the same time, an important epistemic advance, to extend the meanings of these words, and to modify them appropriately, so that they become applicable in a certain manner ... to all acts, whether or not they are interwoven with expressive acts.

The interpretation is, however, not entirely correct. Husserl

[4] 'Der Gedanke', p. 74.
[5] *Ideen*, §124.

draws a distinction between two ingredients of the noema of a mental act: that which is capable of being expressed in words, for which he sometimes uses the phrase "the noematic sense", and which forms what he calls the 'nucleus' or 'core' of the noema; and those ingredients which are not so expressible, which form the outer layers of the full noema. Thus he says in *Ideen*:[6]

> Each of these experiences is "inhabited" by a noematic sense, and however closely related this may be in different experiences, indeed essentially the same as regards the constitution of the nucleus, it is nevertheless variegated in experiences of different kinds.... We observe from this that we must separate from within the *full* noema ... *essentially different strata*, which group themselves around a *central* "*nucleus*", around the pure "*objectual sense*" – around that which ... is describable simply by identical objective expressions, because it could be something identical in parallel experiences of different kinds.

Elsewhere in the same work[7] he states explicitly that:

> Each thing "intended [*Gemeinte*] as such", each intention [*Meinung*] in the noematic sense of any act whatever (indeed, as its noematic nucleus) is *expressible through "meanings"*.... "Expression" is a remarkable form, which allows itself to be adapted to every "sense" (to the noematic "nucleus") and raises it to the realm of "logos", of the *conceptual* and thereby of the *universal*.

By "meanings" Husserl here plainly intends "linguistic meanings". Thus a noema consists, in its central core, of a sense that can be expressed linguistically, but is not, in general, present as so expressed in the mental act which it informs. The noema comprises, further, outer layers not claimed to be expressible in language. In the section from which the first quotation was taken, Husserl is principally

[6] Ibid., §91.
[7] §124.

interested in that component of these outer layers that give the act what he calls its 'character', that is, make it the kind of act it is: an act of perception, of memory, of imagination, and so on; it is not clear whether seeing someone come in and hearing someone come in have the same or different characters. Mental acts of these and many other kinds may have a noematic sense or central core in common. The truth in this is that these 'acts' all are, or at least may be, what in the analytic tradition are called 'propositional attitudes'. We remember *that* something is so, which we formerly perceived to be so, while, perhaps, others merely visualise it as being so, or wonder whether it is so, or fear that it may be so. The character thus corresponds to the 'quality' in the earlier terminology, and stands to the nucleus in a relation vaguely analogous to that in which what Frege called 'force' stands to a Fregean sense; but Husserl's notion is far more general. The analogy is weak in that, for Frege, the force attached to an utterance served to convey what the speaker was *doing* with the thought he was expressing – asserting it to be true, asking after its truth, or the like; but the character of being a visual perception can hardly be described as something the subject is doing with the noematic sense that informs that act. Character can hardly be the only one of the outer layers of the noema; but Husserl does not help us very much to understand what the others are.

Sketchy as was Frege's account of sense-perception, there seems to be considerable similarity between it and Husserl's: both regard an act of perception as informed by a sense expressible in words. Frege's theory is hobbled by his commitment to the thesis that thoughts are accessible to us only through language. If this means that we can grasp thoughts only by understanding sentences expressing them, we obtain a very implausible theory of sense-perception; but, if we set any such contention aside, we are left with no explanation of how we grasp those thoughts that open up the external world to us in perception. But Husserl's theory is not in better but in worse case. His notion of meaning was not, indeed, connected at the outset with the senses of words, and so can be thought to be detachable; but that only underlines the lack of any substantial account of what it is. We should expect the veridicality of the perception or memory, the realisation of the fear or satisfaction of the hope, and so on, to be explicable as the truth of a judgement or proposition contained within the noematic sense; but we do not know how the constituent meanings combine to constitute a state of affairs as intentional object, since they are not, like Frege's senses, by their very essence aimed at truth. We do not know *why* all noematic senses are capable of being expressed in language; and, although it is clear that they are detachable from language, we do not know how we grasp them, or, hence, what exactly the noetic ingredient in an act of sensory perception is (Smith's 'linkage problem').

To understand more clearly what Husserl had in mind, let us consider the question, "What *is* the noema of an act of sense-perception?", without paying excessive attention to the question of expressibility. It would be a complete mistake to equate the noema with the sense-impressions ingredient in the perceptual act. These are collectively called 'hyle' by Husserl, and his view of them is the same as Frege's. The noema is what renders the perceptual act one that has an object, and hence is something that points beyond itself to an object in the external world; sense-impressions, on the other hand, do not, in themselves, point to anything beyond – we simply *have* them. "In themselves" here means 'considered as such', rather than 'when isolated from their accompaniments': we cannot have sense-impressions uninformed by any noema, or, if we can, we are not then perceiving anything; and, in the normal case of genuine perception, the sense-impressions cannot be isolated from the act in which they are integrated with the noema. The noema must have the following properties: it is that which renders the perception *of* an object; it may be a common ingredient of different acts of perception, just as a sense may be the sense of different utterances; and it may vary while the object remains the same, just as there may be different senses with the same reference. It consists, therefore, in the first instance, in our apprehending our sense-impressions as representations of an external object. For the use of a linguistic expression to achieve reference to an object, there must be that in its sense which, together with the circumstances of its use, constitutes a particular object as its referent. Now, for his act of perception to have a genuine external object, the perceiver must perceive some particular object; and it might well be thought that, in the same way as with linguistic sense, the noema must involve whatever is required to make the perceptual act a perception of just that object. There must, of course, be an account of what makes a particular object that which is, at a given time, being perceived by a particular subject. We should not normally take that as problematic, but as explicable in causal terms: the object perceived is that which gives rise to our sense-impressions. But, for Husserl, what determines the object of perception, like what determines the object of any other mental act, is internal to the act, that is, intrinsic to the noema which informs that act. In the same way, what determines what object is being spoken of or thought about is, on a Fregean account, internal to the thought expressed or entertained: the object of discussion or consideration is the referent of the sense associated with the singular term used or constitutive of the thought. Any causal connection is therefore irrelevant.

More exactly, it is irrelevant in all cases save those in which the concept of causality is involved in the relevant sense, as when I think of someone as the person my noticing whom initiated my present train of thought. It would be possible to hold that the noema informing any act of perception always involved reference to a particular object via the notion of causality, namely as being the cause of the subject's sense-impressions. But, so far as I have understood him, Husserl neither proposes this as a solution nor engages in any other especial effort to explain what makes a *particular* object that towards which a given act of perception is directed. In Investigation VI of the *Logische Untersuchungen*, he had devoted some attention to the use of a demonstrative phrase like "that blackbird" in what he calls a 'perceptual statement', that is, a report of present observation. But, in his later treatment, his concern, when discussing the noema of such an act appears to be wholly concentrated upon the perceiver's apprehension of the object, not merely as an external object, but as (currently) having certain general characteristics. The necessity that an act of perception involve a noema amounts to the requirement that we always perceive an object *as* having such characteristics: as being of a certain kind, say, or as having a certain three-dimensional shape or again as disposed to behave in certain ways.

In some passages, Husserl carries this very far. Here is one from the posthumously published *Erfahrung und Urteil*:[8]

> The factual world of experience is experienced as a *typified world*. Things are experienced as trees, bushes, animals, snakes, birds; specifically, as pine, lime-tree, lilac, dog, viper, swallow, sparrow and so on. The table is characterised as being familiar and yet new.

I take it that Husserl here means that it is new, in that that particular table has not been seen before, but familiar in being a *table*. He continues:

> What is given in experience as a new individual is first known in terms of what has been genuinely perceived; it calls to mind the like (the similar). But what is apprehended *according to type* also has a horizon of possible experience with corresponding prescriptions of familiarity and has, therefore, *types* of attributes not yet experienced be expected. When we see a dog, we immediately anticipate its additional modes of behaviour: its typical ways of eating, playing, running, jumping and so on. We do not actually see its teeth: but we know in advance how its teeth will look – not in their individual determination but *according to type*, inasmuch as we have already had previous and frequent experience with similar animals, with dogs, that they have such things as teeth and of this typical kind.

[8] E. Husserl, *Erfahrung und Urteil*, Prague, 1938; Hamburg, ed. L. Landgrabe, 1948, Part III, Chap. I, §83(a), pp. 398-9; English trans. by J. Churchill and K. Ameriks, *Experience and Judgment*, Evanston, 1973, p. 331.

In a visual perception of a dog, then, the noema renders the perception intrinsically that *of a dog*, in that, even were it illusory, a characterisation of the perceptual experience would have to include its being of a dog. In such a case, it is therefore embodied in the noema that informs the visual impressions that what I am seeing is a dog. Now one first reaction to this passage might be that Husserl's account of perception in Logical Investigation VI would fit the case much better. However much our recognition of the animal as a dog, and, indeed, of the object as an animal, may, in experience, form some kind of unity with our perception of it, the two are distinguishable acts: registering what is seen as a dog is, on this view, a mere conceptual *accompaniment* of the act of perception, a judgement *prompted* by it but not inseparable from it.

Let us set that question aside for the time being. What plainly cannot be detached, even conceptually, from the perception is the percipient's apprehension of the three-dimensional shape of the object, including, of course, that part of it not actually presently accessible to the senses, its orientation and its rough distance from him. To these we should, I think, add his impression of its rigidity and cohesion: whether it is something that will disperse, like a puff of smoke, flow, like water or treacle, droop, like a piece of string, or remain in its present shape if not subjected to pressure; and whether, like an animal or a functioning machine, it will move of itself or only under external forces. These, and further characters that might be added, all have to do, as Husserl says, with the expectations generated by the act of perception. We should note, in particular, that the shape the object is taken to have governs other expectations than those usually mentioned in this connection, namely how it will look from other positions. It also governs expectations concerning its behaviour, for instance whether it will stand upon a flat horizontal surface if placed on it with one or another orientation; for our apprehension of the world as revealed to us in sense-perception is guided, from a very early stage of our lives, both by a basic classification of types of substance according to their behaviour and by a rudimentary terrestrial physics and geometry. All this, then, may at least plausibly be reckoned as belonging to the noema in something akin to Husserl's conception of it, and, presumably, to the central nucleus.

CHAPTER 12

Proto-Thoughts

It would nowadays be rather generally accepted that a large part of our seeing an object *as* of this or that shape or nature is integral to the act of visual perception, and likewise for the other senses; what is obscure is the account to be given of seeing *as*. Plainly it has much to do with the expectations generated by the perception: equally plainly, it is not simply a matter of having these expectations or those, since the well-known voluntary or involuntary switch of aspect of a picture, such as the Necker cube and many others, can hardly be explained in that way. Our present question is whether the notion of *sense* assists us here, and, if so, how. Both Frege and Husserl surely went too far in assimilating the 'interpretation' whose informing our sensations constitutes our sense-perceptions to the thoughts that we express in language. For Frege, it simply *consisted* in such thoughts, to which, moreover, he believed that we human beings have access only through language; for Husserl, it consisted in part in meanings that are completely expressible in language – probably by whole sentences, although he left this unclear – and in part of meanings in a generalised sense that are not so expressible. But we are in fact here operating at a level below that of thought as expressible in words; at that level, namely, at which animals devoid of language operate. Frege pointed out, in effect, that we cannot attribute to a dog such a thought as 'There is only one dog barring my way', because he does not

have the concept 'one'.[1] He observed, however, that this does
not mean that the dog is unable to distinguish between being
attacked by one hostile dog and by several. He might well, for
example, have adopted a policy of standing his ground on a
particular route when there was only one hostile dog about,
but of retreating whenever there was more than one, and do
what we should find it difficult to describe otherwise than as
'looking about to make sure that there was only one'.
Nevertheless, as Frege remarked, the dog has no "consciousness, however dim, of that common element which we express
by the word 'one' between the cases, for example, in which he
is bitten by *one* larger dog and in which he chases *one* cat";
and this blocks us from seriously ascribing to him the
thought, 'There is only one dog there'. He has, we may say,
proto-thoughts, which cannot be accurately expressed in
language, because any sentence that suggests itself is
conceptually too rich for the purpose.

Perhaps the least difficult case for the characterisation of
such proto-thoughts, at least as we engage in them, is the
purely spatial one. A car driver or a canoeist may have rapidly
to estimate the speed and direction of oncoming cars or boats
and their probable trajectory, consider what avoiding action
to take, and so on: it is natural to say that he is engaged in
highly concentrated thought. But the vehicle of such thoughts
is certainly not language: it should be said, I think, to consist
in visual imagination superimposed on the visually perceived
scene. It is not just that these thoughts are not in fact framed
in words: it is that they do not have the structure of verbally
expressed thoughts. But they deserve the name of 'proto-
thought' because, while it would be ponderous to speak of
truth and falsity in application to them, they are intrinsically
connected with the possibility of their being mistaken:
judgement, in a non-technical sense, is just what the driver
and the canoeist need to exercise.

Proto-thought is distinguished from full-fledged thought, as
engaged in by human beings for whom language is its vehicle,

[1] *Die Grundlagen der Arithmetik*, §31.

by its incapacity for detachment from present activity and circumstances. A human being may be suddenly struck by a thought, which might be the key to the solution of a mathematical problem or the fact that he has left some vital document at home: in the latter case, he may turn round and go back for it. An animal, or, for that matter, an infant, cannot act in that way. Our thoughts may float free of the environment: we may follow a train of thought quite irrelevant to our surroundings or what we are engaged in doing. An animal may solve quite complex problems, by a process of thinking out the solution, as was illustrated by Köhler's chimpanzees, or by the pony which, confronted by a cattle-grid, lay down and rolled over it: but its thought, or, more exactly, proto-thought, cannot float free, but can occur only as integrated with current activity. This limitation is presumably due to the fact, as I have suggested, that its vehicle consists in spatial images superimposed on spatial perceptions. The driver and the canoeist may likewise solve quite complex problems, and with great rapidity: but their thought will largely be conducted at the pre-linguistic level which permits of such intellectual activity only as integrated into present action. It is difficult for us to recognise in ourselves the operation of this faculty just because we slide so readily from proto-thought to full-fledged thought whose vehicle is language: but we cannot give a good account of our basic ability to apprehend and move about the world if we overlook it. Just that mistake is involved in the suggestion once made by A.J. Ayer that it is by acquiring language that the infant learns to conceive of the world as a spatially three-dimensional one in which he is located.

We ought therefore to respond to Frege's thesis that we can without contradiction conceive of beings who think just the same thoughts as we do, without clothing them in language, by allowing that there may be a non-linguistic activity closely resembling thinking, but denying that it will necessarily issue in thoughts accurately expressible in language. Thoughts, or something akin to thoughts, do not have to have a linguistic vehicle, but they could not occur without a vehicle of any kind;

if we allowed that they could, it is hard to see how we could explain what it is for a thought to have a vehicle, or how we could *ever* be said to think *in* words.

The sublinguistic level of proto-thought is essentially spatial, and therefore must be conceived as operating in our apprehension of what we perceive as having a three-dimensional shape and occupying a three-dimensional position. But it is also essentially dynamic: it involves the apprehension of the possibilities and probabilities of movement, and of the effect of impact. For this reason, it incorporates, not merely perception of position, shape and movement, but also recognition of the gross properties of material things. It is an immediate feature of even our visual perceptions that we observe objects as differentiated according to the general type of material of which they consist: whether they are rigid or flexible, elastic, brittle or plastic, cohesive like a lump of sugar or a heap of grains like caster sugar, solid, liquid or gaseous, wet or dry, smooth or rough, greasy or clean, and so forth. The reason that we use visual clues to project these properties, even though unaided vision does not disclose them, is precisely that they bear on the dynamic possibilities: and so they, too, must be admitted as components of the proto-thoughts which, according to the present proposal, must be taken as fulfilling the role of the noema which Husserl believed to inform our sense-impressions so as to constitute our perceptions.

Is it possible to attribute to the scope of proto-thought concepts, such as that of a dog, as specific as those ascribed by Husserl, in the passage quoted on p. 118, to the noema of a perception, or is it right to view Husserl as here confusing the perception itself with full-fledged thoughts prompted by it? The difficulty in deciding the matter lies in the enormous familiarity of the types of object which, for the most part, we perceive; one cannot see a lamp-post, a rabbit, a car, a tree, a door-knob, a daisy, a spoon or a cloud without immediately recognising it for what it is. It should, however, be remarked that what Husserl says about our perception of the dog could with considerable show of reason be said about a cat's perception of it; for the cat certainly gives every appearance of having as definite expectations of the probable behaviour of the dog, and of the kind of teeth it has in its mouth, as does any human being. The question is not precisely whether we may ascribe to the cat possession of crude versions of such concepts as 'dog' and 'bird'. It is not merely that the cat does not acknowledge such a fundamental principle as that nothing is a dog which is not the offspring of dogs, or that it may fail to classify a penguin, an ostrich or even an eagle as a bird, but that it does not have any concepts, properly so called, at all. It does not have any concepts, because it cannot perform the operations upon concepts that a language-user can perform: it cannot have the thought that all dogs are hairy, or wonder whether there are any exceptions to this generalisation, or reflect that some dogs are hairier than others. But, as thoughts involve concepts, so proto-thoughts involve proto-concepts; our question is, therefore, whether a proto-thought can have the recognition of something as a dog as an ingredient in the same way as it can have the recognition of something as rigid or flexible. It appears to me that it surely can: that Husserl was right in thinking that it may be taken as embracing the recognition of *types* of object with characteristic behaviour that are familiar in our experience and evoke specific behavioural responses on our part.

To invoke Husserl's authority for this view is of course tendentious, in that he was not distinguishing thought from proto-thought, but regarded the central nucleus of the noema as expressible in language without distortion, while leaving it to be supposed that the surrounding strata are not so expressible. This, however, is the fundamental weakness of his account, as also of Frege's. Both their treatments of sense-perception approach what must be the truth of the matter. They were obviously right to hold that perception is not simply a matter of sensation, but that it has a further component at least analogous to thought. But neither account is acceptable as it stands. Frege simply identified the further component with thought, whereas Husserl wanted to explain it by generalising the notion of sense; but the one failed to show how thoughts could be fused with sensations, while the other failed to make clear how the notion of sense was capable of generalisation.

What shows, more sharply than the internal weaknesses of these two accounts, that neither can be accepted as it stands is the impossibility of adapting them to explain the perceptual processes of animals or of infants not yet in possession of language. We cannot say that animals are locked into their inner worlds of sensation and are unable to attain an awareness of physical reality; yet we have seen that thoughts of the kind that are expressible in language cannot be attributed to them. It is a mistake to suppose that because, by means of language, we can engage in thought-processes both far richer and more precise than those of which animals are capable, we do not also engage in ones very similar to theirs. A cat can perceive a dog just as a human being can: there is no good reason to suppose that utterly different accounts should be given of feline and of human perceptions of such an object. To attain an adequate account of perception, thought in the full-fledged sense has to be differentiated from the proto-thought of which animals without language are capable, and in which we, too, must be regarded as frequently engaging, voluntarily and involuntarily, and the difficult task undertaken of saying clearly in what such proto-thought consists.

CHAPTER 13

Thought and Language

(i) The philosophy of thought

Much of the foregoing discussion may have seemed remote from our initial enquiry into the origins of analytical philosophy. If we identify the linguistic turn as the starting-point of analytical philosophy proper, there can be no doubt that, to however great an extent Frege, Moore and Russell prepared the ground, the crucial step was taken by Wittgenstein in the *Tractatus Logico-philosophicus* of 1922. We have been concerned, however, with the preparation of the ground. Before the philosophy of language could be seen, not as a minor specialised branch of the subject, but as the stem from which all other branches grow, it was first necessary that the fundamental place should be accorded to the philosophy of thought. That could not happen until the philosophy of thought had been disentangled from philosophical psychology; and that in turn depended upon the step that so perplexed Brentano, the extrusion of thoughts from the mind and the consequent rejection of psychologism. The step was taken by Frege and by the Husserl of the *Logische Untersuchungen*, who had been so deeply influenced by Bolzano, if not, as many have argued, by Frege himself. Frege was the first philosopher in history to achieve anything resembling a plausible account of the nature of thoughts and of their inner structure. His account depended upon his conviction of the parallelism between thought and language. His interest was in thought, not in language for its own sake:

he was concerned with those features of language irrelevant to the expression of thought only in order to set them aside. Nevertheless, his strategy for analysing thought was to analyse the forms of its linguistic or symbolic expression. Although he continued to reiterate that it is inessential to thoughts and thought-constituents that we grasp them as the senses of sentences and their parts respectively, it is unclear that his account of the senses of linguistic expressions is capable of being transposed into an account of thoughts considered independently of their expression in words. When philosophers consciously embraced the strategy that Frege had pursued, the linguistic turn was thereby decisively taken.

Once the linguistic turn had been taken, the fundamental axiom of analytical philosophy – that the only route to the analysis of thought goes through the analysis of language – naturally appeared compelling. Acceptance of that axiom resulted in the identification of the philosophy of thought with the philosophy of language, or, to give it a grander title, with the theory of meaning; at that stage, analytical philosophy had come of age. Davidson affords an extraordinarily clear example of the fact that, for analytical philsophers faithful to the fundamental axiom, the theory of meaning is indeed fundamental to philosophy as a whole: his writings on a remarkably large range of topics start with an exposition of his general views on the form of a theory of meaning, and go on to draw consequences from them for the topic in hand. Wittgenstein, by contrast, in his later writings eschewed any general *theory* of meaning, believing that any attempt at a systematic account of language must force diverse phenomena into a single form of description which would perforce distort many of them, and that therefore only a piecemeal approach is possible: but he, too, believed that the aim of all philosophy is to enable us to see the world aright by attaining a commanding view of the workings of our language, and hence of the structure of our thought.

The phrase "the philosophy of thought" is an unfamiliar one, although it is becoming more common through the work of Evans and of his followers such as Peacocke, philosophers in the analytical tradition who have rejected the fundamental axiom. From the present point of view, they have not retreated very far, because, although they no longer give the same fundamental place to language, they still treat the philosophy of thought as the foundation of philosophy, so that the general architecture of the subject remains essentially the same for them as for those who still adhere to the fundamental axiom.

The philosophy of thought is that part of philosophy to which, apart from the philosophy of mathematics, Frege devoted his principal attention: he himself referred to it as 'logic', but this term, even with the prefix 'philosophical', is best reserved for what has to do with deductive inference. The philosophy of thought concerns itself with the question what it is to have a thought, and with the structure of thoughts and their components: what it is for a thought to be about an object of one or another kind, what it is to grasp a concept and how a concept can be a component of a thought. Concern with such questions has, indeed, been manifested by philosophers for a very long time and by those of very diverse schools: but the philosophy of thought could not emerge as a distinguishable sector of the subject until it had been disentangled from the general philosophy of mind. As already remarked, that could happen only after the step had been taken of extruding thoughts from the mind; and this step, taken not only by Frege as the grandfather of analytical philosophy, but equally by Husserl as the founder of phenomenology, was therefore one of two that had to be taken before any plausible answer could be given to the question, "What is a thought?". The other has been barely touched on in this book. Expressed in linguistic terms, it consists in acknowledging the primacy of the sentence in an account of meaning: an explanation of the meaning of a word is required to determine the contribution that a word makes to the meanings of sentences containing it, and is required to do nothing else than that.

Expressed in terms of thought rather than of language, the principle is that of the primacy of complete thoughts over their constituent senses, that is, a weakened version of what was earlier called the dependence thesis, namely that such a sense can be grasped only as a potential common part of different complete thoughts. (The dependence thesis proper required it to be an *actual* part of some particular complete thought.) As Frege perceived, a complete thought is to be characterised as that which it makes sense to qualify as true or as false: the connection between sense and truth-value has therefore to be made from the outset if any plausible answer to the question, "What is a thought?", is to be given.

It was Frege who first clearly posed the question, "What is it to have a thought?", as one demanding a non-psychological answer, and it was he who first attempted to supply a substantive answer to it. A curious fragment among his posthumously published papers, consisting of seventeen brief numbered remarks, may shed an unexpected light upon his intellectual development.[1] They prove to be a sequence of comments on the Introduction to Lotze's *Logik*, published in 1874. We tend to think of Frege as a mathematical logician – the first mathematical logician – who was gradually drawn into philosophy in the course of carrying out, and providing arguments to justify, his project of founding number theory and analysis upon pure logic. It is my belief, however, that Frege's comments on Lotze's *Logik* were written before his *Begriffsschrift* of 1879 was composed, and thus represent the earliest piece of philosophical writing from his pen that has come down to us. If I am right, they show that he was interested in general philosophical questions long before he attempted to build logical foundations for arithmetic; and the question on which his comments on Lotze centre is "What is a thought?". Here we already find a denial that logical laws can be established by psychological investigations, a sharp distinction made between thoughts and combinations of ideas, the possibility of being true or false singled out as the distinguishing mark of a thought, and even the thesis that

[1] G. Frege, 'Siebzehn Kernsätze zur Logik', *Posthumous Writings*, pp. 174-5. See M. Dummett, 'Frege's "Kernsätze zur Logik" ', *Inquiry*, Vol. 24, 1981, pp. 439-48; reprinted in M. Dummett, *Frege and Other Philosophers*, Oxford, 1991.

truth is indefinable. Among Frege's strictly philosophical preoccupations, as opposed to those relating more particularly to mathematics, the quest for a characterisation of thoughts and of what distinguishes them from the contents of consciousness properly so called was both the earliest and the most enduring.

(ii) The code conception of language

The extrusion of thoughts from the mind initiated by Bolzano led to what is often termed 'platonism', as exemplified by Frege's mythology of the 'third realm': for, if thoughts are not contents of the mind, they must be located in a compartment of reality distinct both from the physical world and the inner world of private experience. This mythology served Frege and Husserl as a bulwark against the psychologism which they opposed. If, now, our capacity for thought is equated with, or at least explained in terms of, our ability to use language, no such bulwark is required: for language is a social phenomenon, in no way private to the individual, and its use is publicly observable. It is for this reason that the linguistic turn may be seen as a device for continuing to treat thoughts as objective and utterly disparate from inner mental events, without having recourse to the platonistic mythology. There is therefore danger in reversing the priority of language over thought, in the manner of Evans and others: the danger of falling back into psychologism. Now, for Frege, the principal crime of psychologism was that it makes thoughts subjective, and hence incommunicable. We have seen, however, that even if there were incommunicable thoughts – as Frege found himself reluctantly constrained to concede that there are – such thoughts would still not be contents of consciousness; it follows that the extrusion of thoughts from the mind does not rest solely upon the argument from objectivity.

Now it can sound perverse to maintain that thoughts are not items of consciousness: thoughts, and fragments of thoughts, are, after all, precisely what novelists who have tried to depict a stream of consciousness have represented it as composed of. Thoughts are regularly spoken of as 'occurring' to people: this is why we are bound to admit an occurrent notion of grasping a thought. The force of denying that thoughts are mental contents is clearly seen, however, when we consider the code conception of language, very accurately expressed in the following passage from Saussure:[2]

> Suppose there are two people, A and B, talking to one another. The circuit begins in the brain of one of them, say A, in which the objects of consciousness, which we may call concepts, are located, associated with representations of the linguistic signs, or auditory images, that serve to express them. We may suppose that a given concept releases in the brain a corresponding auditory image; this is an entirely *psychic* phenomenon, followed in turn by a *physiological* process: the brain transmits an impulse corresponding to the image to the organs of sound production; the sound-waves are then propagated from the mouth of A to the ear of B: a purely *physical* process. Next, the circuit continues in B, in the reverse order: from the ear to the brain, a physiological transmission of the auditory image; in the brain, the psychic association of this image with the corresponding concept.

This account of the process of communication is plainly untenable. It imitates the associationist account put forward by the British empiricists: but they identified concepts with ideas, which they typically understood as mental images. The conception of an established association between such mental images and auditory images or impressions is not in itself absurd: what was wrong in their account was the representation of concepts – the meanings of words – as mental images in the first place. But someone's understanding a word as expressing a certain concept cannot be explained as consisting in the word's calling up in his mind a concept with which he has come to associate it, since there is no such process as a concept's coming into anyone's mind: a tune, a name, a remembered scene or scent can come into the

---

[2] F. de Saussure, *Cours de linguistique générale*, ed. T. de Mauro, Paris, 1985, pp. 17-18.

mind, but a concept is not the sort of thing of which this can intelligibly be said. Even were the concept one that only that individual could grasp, so that it could not be communicated to another, it would still not be the sort of thing that could be said to come into the mind. True enough, as we have seen, we must admit an occurrent sense of taking a word as having a certain meaning, since an ambiguous word may be taken by the same individual on one occasion as having one of its two meanings and on another occasion as having the other: we therefore need an account of what it is to take a word, on a given occasion, as having a particular meaning. This will not, however, be provided in the simple-minded manner suggested by Saussure. If to have a concept were to be like having an intermittent pain, in that the concept came to mind on certain occasions, we should still need an explanation of what it was to *apply* that concept. Someone incapable of applying it would ordinarily be judged simply to lack the concept, just as someone incapable of telling whether something was or was not a tree, or of saying anything about what trees are or do, would be judged ignorant of the meaning of the word "tree": it would be useless for him to claim that, whenever he heard the word, the concept of a tree came into his mind, although this happened to be a concept that he could not apply. Rather, his ability to apply the concept *constitutes* his having that concept: it makes no difference whether, when he applies it, anything comes into his mind in the manner in which a tune might do so; and, for that reason, whatever did come into his mind would not *be* the concept.

What Frege called 'senses' were for him both the salient ingredients of the meanings of words and the constituent parts of thoughts. The senses at least of general terms are obviously closely connected with the concepts of which Saussure speaks: a word may express a certain concept, and one who understands it as expressing that concept has grasped its sense. It is because concepts cannot be spoken of as coming into the mind as do mental images that they cannot be described as contents of consciousness; and it is precisely this that gives the strongest ground for believing the fundamental axiom of analytical philosophy, that is, that the analysis of thought both can and must go via the analysis of its linguistic expression. For, if we cannot characterise a grasp of the meaning of a word as the association of the appropriate concept with the word, then, even if the subject be supposed to possess the concept before he learns the word, we cannot make *use* of this hypothesis in explaining in what his understanding of the word consists. It may be, indeed, that abilities that manifest his pre-linguistic grasp of the concept must also be possessed by anyone who is to be said to understand the word, the exercise of these abilities forming part of any use of the word adequate for the ascription of a full understanding of it. In that case, however, the description of this use can be made explicit without any appeal to his prior grasp of the concept; and this description will itself make manifest in what a grasp of the concept consists. It thus appears that an account of linguistic meaning cannot rest upon any conception of the thoughts which the speaker may have been capable of having, or the concepts which he may have grasped, antecedently to his acquisition of language; an explanation of linguistic meanings will be incapable of exploiting the assumption that the speaker already had thoughts of the kind he learns to express in words when he first learns language. Rather, in explaining linguistic meaning, we shall thereby be explaining what it is to have such thoughts. Since, however, there are many thoughts which are evidently inaccessible to creatures without any means of manipulating linguistic or symbolic tokens, and since all thoughts are more perspicuously articulated in language than through any other means of expression, a theory of meaning for a language supplies the only means we have for attaining an account of thoughts adequate for the range of human thought in general.

It is because concepts, in this sense, cannot be spoken of as coming into the mind as ideas can that they cannot be described as contents of consciousness. Now a thought cannot be grasped save as a complex: having a thought is one mode of activation of the ability which comprises a grasp of any one of the concepts the thought involves. It is not merely that thoughts must obey what Evans calls the 'generality constraint', for example, that no one could have the thought, 'This rose smells sweet', without knowing (roughly) what roses are, or without being capable of having other thoughts about that rose, or without an awareness of what it is for other things to smell sweet or for something not to smell sweet.[3] It is that no one can have such a thought without apprehending its complexity, that is, in this example, without conceiving of himself as thinking about the rose, and as thinking of it something that can be true of other things and false of yet others.

(iii) Are thoughts contents of consciousness?

How, then, can we get from the premiss that concepts are not contents of consciousness to the conclusion that thoughts are not contents of consciousness, either? Can we argue that, since a thought is a complex, and the constituents of the complex are not mental contents, the complex itself cannot be a mental content? This does not appear immediately to follow, because the impossibility of a concept's coming into the mind may be explicable by the dependence thesis: a concept cannot exist on its own, nor, therefore, come into the mind on its own, but only *as* a constituent of a thought, which, perhaps, can come to mind. So, although the code conception of language advanced by Saussure must be rejected, Frege's denial that *thoughts* are mental contents still appears to await grounds.

In posing these questions, we have slid into identifying the concept expressed by a word with its sense, and this is not quite right: rather, a grasp of the sense of the word is one manifestation of a possession of the concept. More damagingly, we have reverted to the conception of a sense's being before the mind, if only in combination with other senses to form a complete thought. This is almost inevitable so long as we cling to Frege's mythology; but, having rejected the

---

[3] See G. Evans, *The Varieties of Reference*, pp. 100-5.

mythology, we must reject, with it, the notion of a thought's being before the mind as an object to be inspected. For the fact is that the mythological picture is incoherent. It is perfectly consistent to say both that this lectern is not a content of my mind, but a constituent of physical reality external to it, and that I am aware of it in virtue of its being visually presented to me: for the visual impression constitutes the mode of my awareness. But, as we saw, on Frege's theory it is not merely that a thought which I am entertaining is not a content of my mind, but a constituent of an immaterial reality external to it; it is, further, that my apprehension of the thought is not mediated by anything in my mind: it is, rather, presented to my mind *directly* – and yet it is not a content of my mind. And this conception is not consistent.

Since possession of a concept is an ability, it cannot, of its nature, form anything but a necessary background for having a thought. It was said above that a grasp of the sense of a word is a particular manifestation of possession of the corresponding concept, but this is still not completely accurate. On the dispositional interpretation of 'grasping the sense', it is itself an ability, for instance to recognise the truth or falsity of statements containing the word; and even on the occurrent interpretation, it is more like a propensity to treat or respond to a particular such statement in one way rather than another. A grasp of the sense of a word that expresses a given concept is thus more properly described as a set of abilities forming a species of which possession of the concept is the superordinate genus. It forms the essential background to a grasp of the thought expressed by a sentence, whether heard or uttered, in that the mere utterance of the sentence serves to express the thought, and the mere hearing of the sentence to apprehend it, for one who knows the language, without any further mental activity, subsequent or simultaneous, on his part.

It is because possession of a concept forms the background to an occurrent grasp of a thought – to what we call *having* a thought – that thoughts frequently occur to us otherwise than as expressed by complete sentences. A man reaches in his pocket for his spectacles, fails to find them, and glances at his jacket: a look of consternation comes over his face. We could caption this, "Where are they? Oh, I put on a different suit this morning. I must *again* have forgotten to take them out of my other jacket": but the verbal accompaniment of his train of thought may be very slight, or even non-existent. Even if he had uttered the sentence, "I have left my spectacles in my other jacket," this would have expressed his thought only in virtue of the background, namely his knowledge of the language. It is therefore no mystery that, in the case I imagined, it is the background to his actions, feelings and perceptions that makes it correct to attribute those thoughts to him: his concentration upon the whereabouts of his spectacles, and his having been through a similar sequence before, together suffice to make his memory of having put on a different jacket on the part of one who possesses the relevant concepts a vehicle of the thought. We have here only an extreme case of what happens when someone expresses a complex thought by means of just one or two words, to himself (as in a note for a speech) or to another who knows him very well or has discussed the topic with him. All this serves to clarify the notion of a content of the mind with which we have been operating: it is something whose presence is independent of all background circumstances. The thought that he had left his spectacles in his other jacket genuinely occurs to the subject in our example at the moment when his look of bewilderment changes to one of irritation: but it, too, is not the kind of thing that can be a content of the mind in the sense now made explicit.

(iv) Thought as prior to language

Such cases, of barely verbalised or even quite unverbalised thinking, increase the attraction of what is in any case more natural, namely a reversed strategy which explains language in terms of thoughts, conceived as grasped independently of language, rather than conversely: for if possession of the relevant concepts is sufficient as a background for having a given thought, and if it is possible to manifest possession of those concepts in non-linguistic behaviour, then, after all, it will be possible to explain what it is to have that thought without appeal to its linguistic expression. Such a strategy of philosophical explanation, long advocated by Roderick Chisholm, will, of course, need to avoid falling back into the illegitimate code conception of language, illustrated by the quotation from Saussure. This can, however, be done by repudiating Frege's identification of the senses of words with the corresponding thought-constituents. On such a view, an understanding of a sentence, or, better, of a particular utterance of it, may involve the hearer's recognising that he is required to have a certain thought (not, of course, to accept it as true); the significance of a word occurring in the sentence will then be that of a signal circumscribing the thought he is required to have, rather than of a representation of the corresponding constituent of that thought.

It is this approach of which it was earlier remarked that it stood in danger of falling into the psychologism Frege and Husserl were so anxious to avoid. It is not my intention here to discuss in any detail the complex issue of the priority, in respect of philosophical explanation, as between thought and language. My argument for distinguishing thoughts proper from proto-thoughts turned on the unavailability to a creature devoid of language of many of the concepts expressible in language: which thoughts, properly so called, are ascribable to a languageless being will then depend upon a careful investigation of the concepts he can be supposed to possess. It is obvious, as an empirical fact, that, while a dog can remember where he hid a bone and a squirrel where he deposited his hoard of nuts, neither can suddenly realise that he must have left something somewhere. The fundamental reason for this is clearly that such animals do not have a memory for specific past events, as we do; and this in turn follows from their not having the concepts required for locating events in past time. It is at least plausible that such concepts are accessible only by those who have a language that includes some scheme of dating, absolute or relative to the present: if so, a thought of the kind, 'I have left my spectacles in my other jacket', though it can occur quite unverbalised, is unavailable to any but a language-user.

The true ground for Frege's doctrine, shared by Bolzano and by Husserl, that thoughts and their constituent senses are not mental contents thus lies in their categorial difference from mental images and sense-impressions, rather than where Frege located it, in the objectivity of thought and the subjectivity of the mental. The mythology of the 'third realm', constructed to defend the doctrine, actually undermines it, however: our apprehension of thoughts must be unmediated, whereas that of which we have an unmediated awareness can only be a mental content. Now a theory like that of Evans, which explains language in terms of thought, is in relatively little danger, unless it is very crudely formulated, of ignoring the categorial difference between thoughts and ideas in Frege's sense; but it is in some danger of overlooking the point of Frege's insistence on the communicability of thoughts. This needs some explanation.

(v) The communicability of thoughts

Frege repeatedly drew weaker conclusions about the subjectivity of what he called 'ideas' (*Vorstellungen*) than his arguments would warrant. He inferred from them that we cannot know whether your sense-impression is the same as mine, where he should have inferred that the question is senseless: he stated that we can never completely communicate our ideas and sensations to others, when his arguments imply that we cannot communicate them at all. This points to a certain embarrassment about the correctness of those arguments. The fact of the matter is that his exaggerated belief in the radical subjectivity of 'ideas' sprang from a failure to apply his own doctrines to their case; more exactly, from a failure to draw the consequences for epistemology of his philosophy of thought and of language. Knowledge, he once remarked in passing, issues in judgements.[4] A judgement is,

[4] G. Frege, 'Logik' (1897), *Posthumous Writings*, p. 144.

in his characterisation, an 'advance from a thought to a truth-value'.[5] Judgements, and therefore knowledge, are accordingly subject to the same constraints as thoughts: if thoughts are intrinsically communicable, then judgements must be intrinsically communicable, and hence any knowledge we can have must be communicable. Frege's retreat, in 'Der Gedanke', to a notion of incommunicable thoughts was a mistake.[6] It is true that, if I say to you, "I have been wounded", there is a sense in which you cannot *think* the thought that I express. If you think, 'I, too, have been wounded,' you are not thinking the thought that I expressed, on Frege's use of the term "thought", since you are thinking about a different person and hence your thought is one that might be false when mine was true. If, on the other hand, you think, 'Dummett has been wounded,' you are again not thinking the thought that I expressed, since you are not picking me out, as the subject of your thought, in the same way as I did, and so, again, your thought might be false while mine was true, namely if you had misidentified me. In this sense, therefore, Frege was right to say that, for me, the first-person pronoun "I" represents a way in which I am given to myself in which I cannot be given to anyone else. But it does not follow from that that there is something I have necessarily failed to communicate. Although you cannot *think* my thought, you know precisely what thought I was expressing: although you cannot think of me in just that way in which I think of myself when I speak of myself in the first person, you know in which way I was thinking of myself, namely in just that way in which you think of yourself when you speak of *yourself* in the first person.

If what holds good of knowledge holds good also of every type of awareness, then we arrive at the following two conclusions: one cannot think of, and hence cannot be aware

---

[5] G. Frege, 'Über Sinn und Bedeutung', p. 35.

[6] G. Frege, 'Der Gedanke', p. 66: "when Dr. Lauben has the thought that he has been wounded, he probably bases it on the primitive way in which he is given to himself. And only Dr. Lauben himself can grasp thoughts specified in this way. But now he may want to communicate with others. He cannot communicate a thought which only he can grasp."

of, any object save as given in a particular way; and, for any way in which one may think of an object, it must be possible to convey to another the way in which one is thinking of it. These two principles apply, as Frege normally applies them, to objects in the physical world, and, likewise, to the abstract objects which he characterises as objective although not actual. But, since they are quite general, they must also apply to the contents of consciousness: our awareness of inner objects must be mediated by thought, just as is our awareness, in sense-perception, of external objects. It follows that 'ideas', too, must be communicable: despite our incorrigible tendency to believe the opposite, there can be no feature of our sensations that cannot be conveyed to others, although there is a great deal that we do not in fact convey. It is senseless to assert that there is something of which we cannot speak: for, if we cannot speak of it, our attempt to speak of it must necessarily be frustrated. It may be that there is such a thing as having sensations without being aware of them: perhaps this is the condition of various lowly organisms, and it may possibly be the effect of those alarming anaesthetics under which the patient exhibits all the usual pain-reactions, but subsequently avers that he felt nothing. But, for us in a normal state, to have a sensation is to be aware of it, that is, to have thoughts about it; and we therefore cannot attribute sensations such as we have to any creature to which we cannot also ascribe at least proto-thoughts.

To recognise that 'ideas' are communicable, contrary to Frege's opinion, in no way obliterates the distinction between ideas, as being mental contents, and thoughts, as not so being: for the communicability of ideas rests on the communicability of thoughts. More exactly, by saying that ideas are communicable we simply *mean* that thoughts about them are communicable; it would make no sense to say of a mental content that it could be communicated in the way that a thought can be communicated. Nor does a denial that the contents of consciousness are incommunicable, as Frege believed, weaken the force of the attack by him and Husserl upon psychologism; for the psychologism which they opposed agreed with them in regarding psychological operations and the mental contents on which they operate as essentially private. Psychologism of this kind is forced to invoke an *assumption* that the private events occurring in the consciousness of any one subject are essentially similar to those occurring in the consciousness of another: it must represent this as an assumption (or, at best, a probable but untestable hypothesis) precisely because it holds, as Frege did, that there is no way of comparing the two sets of mental events. It may well be, then, that there is no valid conception of the mental according to which the (very similar) arguments of Frege and Husserl against psychologism – those arguments, namely, that turn on the objectivity of sense – prove that sense is not dependent upon psychological processes. It is not, indeed, dependent upon psychological processes; but it may be that the *arguments* they used rested on a false conception of the mental which they shared with the advocates of psychologism. That does not vitiate those arguments, however: for they stand as an enduring bulwark against any conception which would make the senses we attach to expressions, or the concepts we apply, depend upon incommunicable inner processes or states.

Such conceptions are perennially tempting. The best known is that of the private ostensive definition on which each individual is supposed to base the sense he attaches to an expression for an observational property such as a colour. Another is the idea that each assigns meanings to arithmetical expressions by reference to his intuitive grasp of the structure of the natural number system, a grasp which cannot be completely expressed, as Gödel's proof of the incompletability of arithmetic is thought to prove. Any such conception makes communication rest on faith: since whether you understand my words according to the meaning I intended to convey depends on processes within your mind which you cannot communicate and of which I therefore have no knowledge, and since the meaning I intended to convey likewise depends on similar processes within my mind, our belief that we understand one another rests on a faith, which can never be verified, that our mental processes are analogous. Because it rests on faith, this is an unacceptable conception of the intersubjective, which may explain why Frege refused to recognise any category of the intersubjective short of the wholly objective; for a conception which requires faith in the similarity of subjective inner mental operations contradicts the communicability of thoughts. We speak a common language, and we have learned that language solely from what was open to the view of all – the practice of other speakers and their interaction with us, including their correction of our mistakes. All that goes to determine the meanings of the words of that language must therefore likewise be open to view: their meanings cannot depend upon what occurs within our minds, inaccessible to other speakers, and could not depend on that, even if it made sense to speak of such inaccessible inner processes.

Now Evans's programme involves a danger of sliding into just such an illegitimate conception, contradicting the communicability of thought. For when the meanings of words are explained in terms of the kind of thought expressed by the speaker, and the kind of thought which is required of the hearer if he is to understand what the speaker says, there is an inevitable concentration upon what goes on within the minds of the individuals concerned. The meaning of an expression of the common language is objective because it is embodied in the use that a competent speaker is required to make of that expression; but when its meaning is described in terms of the thoughts that speaker and hearer need to have in order to be using it, or understanding it, correctly, the connections with publicly observable use is broken unless public criteria are supplied for someone to have a thought of the required kind.

(vi) The social character of language: the individual character of belief

This is not to argue that an account of language can ignore all that is peculiar to individual speakers in favour of what belongs to a language as a social institution. On the contrary, a delicate balance between individual and social realities is essential to any realistic description of linguistic practice. It is not just that we need to be able to explain the notion of an individual speaker's understanding of his language, an understanding that will in all cases be partial and in some respects faulty; it is that the step from what is meant by what a speaker says to what he believes, wishes or feels goes from social facts to facts about an individual. What a speaker's utterance means depends principally on the correct use of the words in the common language, and only to a minimal extent upon his intentions. But the precise content of the belief that he thereby expresses depends on his personal grasp of those words. This holds true in two obvious ways and one less obvious. The most obvious is that a misunderstanding on someone's part of the meaning of a word of the common language will result in his misstating the belief that he holds; to know what he believes, we must know how he understands the word, not what its true meaning is. Secondly, it is a pervasive feature of our use of language that we exploit the existence of accepted meanings by using words of which we have only an imperfect understanding. If a garage mechanic tells me that the gasket in my car is leaking, I may tell someone else that my car is in the garage having the gasket repaired. I have quite sufficient reason to believe the statement to be true, and may, by making it, transmit sound information, even though I have no clear idea what a gasket is other than that it is a part of a car and can leak. By my utterance, I have undoubtedly *said* that the gasket is being repaired: but I cannot be said to *believe* that the gasket is being repaired, but only that something called the "gasket" is being repaired.

Now in both these cases, the word in question has a meaning in the common language which is known to other speakers, though not to the individual in question: but there are cases in which no one can be said to know everything that constitutes the use of the word in the language. Place-names furnish an excellent example. Someone who had never heard of Bologna, or who knew about it only that it was a city somewhere in Europe, or who knew that it was a place in Italy but did not know whether it was a city, a lake or a mountain, could not be said to know or believe anything about Bologna. If he used the name "Bologna", he would indeed be referring to that city, but he would be in the same position as I in using the word "gasket": no assertion that he made could express more than a belief about a city or place called "Bologna". It is, however, impossible to say how much anyone needs to know about the city named "Bologna" for him to qualify as capable of knowing or believing something about Bologna; more to the point, there is no sense in asking how much someone would have to know in order to know everything that determines the use of the name "Bologna" in the common language. It is certainly relevant to the use of place-names that there are recognised means of getting to the places they name, as it is also relevant that there are recognised means of knowing when you have reached them. This means, first, that not only the institution of maps and atlases, but also that of transport systems and their agencies are part of the entire social practice that gives place-names their use, and, secondly, that, while the name "Bologna" certainly does not mean 'the place called "Bologna" by those who live there', the fact that the name *is* that used by the inhabitants is one strand in the complex which constitutes the use of that name. That is not to say that only those practices which establish the location of a city, mountain or river go to determine its meaning as a term of the common language. Place-names do not differ only according to the kind of thing they name – a city, plain, region or country: they differ also according to whether they name a famous place or a little-known one. The names of very famous cities, such as Athens, Moscow, Delhi or Peking, derive a large part of their significance in the language from the fame of their bearers. No one can count as adequately understanding the name "Rome" if he knows nothing of the Roman Empire or the Papacy: not only must he know these things, but he must also know that they are generally known. That is why the American habit of speaking of "Rome, Italy" is so ludicrous:

there can be only one Rome, that is, only one Rome simpliciter, after which Rome, Ohio, Rome, New York, Rome, Nebraska, and the like are called.

The principal point, however, is that, in the use of place-names, we have an instance of the celebrated phenomenon called by Putnam the 'division of linguistic labour' far more thoroughgoing than those cited by him.[7] His examples were of terms like "gold" and, I may add as a more interesting case, "temperature," which serve both as words of everyday discourse and as technical or theoretical terms, and of which the first use is held responsible to the second: everyday speakers acknowledge that, if a chemist or goldsmith says that a substance is not gold, then it is not. Of such words, some people, namely the experts, know the entire meanings, since they also know the everyday use: it is just that we count ordinary speakers as fully understanding the words, even though they acknowledge the superior authority of the experts over how to apply them. But the use of a place-name is not something that anybody could *know* in its entirety. It is integral to our employment of names of places on the Earth's surface that it is possible, using one or another projection, to draw maps of parts of that surface: and so all the complex techniques of surveying and of map-construction play a part in the web of practices that constitutes our use of place-names. The information relevant to the use of a particular place-name that is provided by maps cannot be reduced to a surveyable list which anyone could learn – say the place's latitude, longitude and height above sea-level. This applies almost equally to what has to do with transport to the place. We have here the clearest of all instances in which the use of language exists only as interwoven with a multitude of non-linguistic practices: the existence of roads and shipping routes, and, in our time, of railways and air flights, and even of travel agencies, enters essentially into the language-game, to use Wittgenstein's phrase, that involves the use of place-names.

[7] Hilary Putnam, 'The Meaning of "Meaning" ', in H. Putnam, *Mind, Language and Reality*, Cambridge, 1975, p. 227.

Here, then, we observe the social character of language at its most prominent. But, when we need to characterise with complete accuracy the belief expressed by a speaker by means of a sentence containing a place-name, our concern will be solely with the connection he personally makes between the name and the place. Normally speaking, of course, we have no reason to trouble to attain such accuracy: it is sufficient that he used the name and that he knows enough to count as able to have a belief about the place. In delicate cases, however, we may need to bother: Kripke's well-known Pierre example provides just such a case.[8]

(vii) The idiolect and the common language

The transition from what an individual speaker says to what he thinks – from what the words he utters mean in the common language to the content of his beliefs – is thus mediated by his personal understanding of the language: and the example of place-names shows that we cannot always equate his understanding of the words he uses with what he takes their meanings in the common language to be. The crucial question is, however, whether we should take the public language or the private understanding of it to be primary. If the approach to the philosophy of thought through the philosophy of language is to serve the purpose of safeguarding the objectivity of thought without a platonistic mythology, language must be conceived as a social institution, as the common possession of the members of a community. This accordingly requires that a theory of meaning should first explain what it is for the expressions of a common language such as Italian, English, Malay, etc., to have the meanings that they do, and only then, by appeal to that explanation, go on to explain in what an individual's grasp of such a language may consist and how it will affect the interpretation of his utterances and the ascription of propositional attitudes to him.

[8] Saul Kripke, 'A Puzzle about Belief', in A. Margalit (ed.), *Meaning and Use*, Dordrecht, 1979.

The alternative is to take as the central notion that of an idiolect, that is, a language as understood by some one individual, explaining first what it is for that individual to attach to the words of his idiolect the meanings that he does, and then characterising a common language as a set of overlapping idiolects. This approach need not take a psychologistic form: in particular, it need not involve a rejection of the fundamental axiom of analytical philosophy, the priority of language over thought in order of explanation. Typically, it will take the form of supposing that a speaker implicitly assumes a theory of meaning for his idiolect. In his celebrated article 'Two Dogmas of Empiricism', Quine presented an image of language as an articulated network of sentences of a wholly individualistic kind: that is to say, the language in question could only be understood as the idiolect of a particular speaker.[9] According to this image, there is, at any one time, a partial function on the sentences of the language, assigning truth-values to them: changes in this function are due jointly to the impact of experience, said to occur only at the periphery of the network, and to the interconnections of sentences within the network, inducing new assignments of truth-values to others. Since no account was taken of disagreements between distinct individuals, or of differences in their experiences, the image could only be understood as intended to represent the changes in the beliefs of a single individual, registered by his acceptance or rejection of the sentences expressing them, under the impact of his personal experiences. Subsequently, in *Word and Object*, Quine modified this image to take account of the social character of language.[10] Many of the notions introduced in that book depend essentially upon there being many speakers of the language. For example, among what Quine calls 'occasion sentences', 'observation sentences' (those giving pure reports

[9] W. V. Quine, 'Two Dogmas of Empiricism', in W. V. Quine, *From a Logical Point of View*, New York, 1963.
[10] Idem., *Word and Object*, Cambridge, Massachusetts, 1960.

of observation) are distinguished by the constancy of their stimulus meanings from one speaker to another (the 'stimulus meaning' of a sentence consisting in the propensity of different sensory stimuli to prompt assent to or dissent from it). The variation, from speaker to speaker, in the stimulus meaning of an occasion sentence that is *not* an observation sentence reflects the differences in the background knowledge possessed by individual speakers. For, although Quine is committed to denying the possibility of disentangling meaning from accepted theory, this applies only to *generally* accepted theory; at least on the account given in *Word and Object*, the knowledge and beliefs of an individual that are not shared by other speakers can be isolated from the meanings that he attaches to his words, on the presumption that those meanings are the ones they bear in the common language. After *Word and Object*, however, Quine has tended to revert to the perspective of 'Two Dogmas', according to which the primary notion is that of an idiolect. The presumption that the meanings a speaker attaches to his words and intends to convey by them are those they have in the common language cannot be maintained according to the later Quine: hence you have what is in principle the same problem of *interpreting* the speech of one who addresses you in your mother-tongue as you do of interpreting utterances in a language of which you are wholly ignorant, even if it is in practice considerably easier to solve. In *Word and Object* two languages were regarded as directly connected if there were any speakers who knew both, or any tradition of translation between them, and indirectly if there existed a chain of languages such that any two successive ones were directly connected; and radical interpretation was then explained as interpretation of a language not even indirectly connected with one's own: but these ideas are at home within a theory which takes the notion of a common language as primary. In Quine's later writings, the notion of an idiolect has assumed the primary role once more: and so radical interpretation must begin at home.

Davidson, too, has moved in the same direction, and has

moved even further.[11] His earliest accounts of a theory of meaning for a language treated the language as the common possession of a community. According to these accounts, the evidence on which any such theory was based consisted in correlations between the sentences – more exactly, the utterances or potential utterances – accepted as true by the speakers and the prevailing circumstances in which they so accepted them. The idea bears an obvious resemblance to Quine's notion of stimulus meaning, although Davidson is making no distinction between types of sentence, and takes all circumstances into account rather than just the sensory stimuli to which the speakers are subject; but, in just the same way, such evidence could hardly be thought to yield a theory of truth for the sentences of the language unless the language were one having a large number of speakers. In his later writings, however, Davidson turned from considering a theory of meaning for such a language to a theory governing an idiolect; since an individual's linguistic habits alter with time, an idiolect had to be considered as the language of a speaker at a given period, whose duration was left unspecified. In his most recent writings, he has gone farther still: since a speaker will use a different vocabulary and diction in addressing different hearers, he no longer takes the unit to be the language of a particular individual at a given time, but, rather, the language in which one particular individual is disposed at a given time to address another particular individual. Such a "language", relativised to two individuals, will again be governed by a theory. When X addresses Y, Y will understand X in accordance with the theory by which he rightly or wrongly presumes X to be governed when speaking to Y; and thus, again, Y will need to engage in interpretation, even if, by ordinary criteria, X and Y are speaking the same language: for Davidson, an utterance has, not a speaker and a hearer, but a speaker and an interpreter.

[11] See Donald Davidson, *Inquiries into Truth and Inerpretation*, Oxford, 1984, and 'A Nice Derangement of Epitaphs' in E. LePore (ed.), *Truth and Interpretation*, Oxford, 1986.

Even Frege, despite his emphasis on the communicability of thoughts by means of language, might be described as giving a theory of sense for an idiolect. This is not to say that anything in his theory of sense *requires* it to apply only to a language as spoken by a single individual; but it is a theory which appears to make no overt appeal to the fact that the language to which it applies has many speakers. The sense of an expression is the way in which its referent is given to one who knows the language: it therefore appears that an individual might attach senses to all the expressions of a language, and thereby understand the sentences of the language as expressing thoughts, without there being anyone else who knew or had ever known that language. As we saw, the notion of force has to do with the use of sentences to say things – to make assertions or ask questions, etc. – and hence their use in communication with others, and so we cannot say that Frege's account of language as a whole is applicable to a language possessed by only one individual: but it comes closer to being so than is comfortable for anyone who believes, as I do, that it is essential to take as primary the notion of a common language and not that of an idiolect.

What, then, is wrong with taking the notion of an idiolect as primary? A first natural objection is that a philosophical account of language that proceeds in this way, though it may not itself be psychologistic, will incur the same objection as that which Frege brought against psychologism: our understanding of others will depend upon untestable hypotheses about the theories of meaning that tacitly guide their utterances. But to this there is a natural retort, namely that such hypotheses will no more be untestable than those formed in the course of genuinely radical interpretation – interpretation of a language not even indirectly connected with one's own. Surely a language that is in fact known to only one person is conceivable: you have only to consider the last surviving speaker of a vanishing language – the last living speaker of Cornish, for example. There could even be a language which only one person had *ever* known. Suppose that an inventor of an artificial language, after the model of

Esperanto, which he calls "Unilingua", works without collaborators, but then never succeeds in persuading anyone to learn it. There would be no difficulty in teaching Unilingua, by the direct method or otherwise: it could even be taught to a child as his mother-tongue. It therefore seems that there can be nothing in principle inconsistent in considering a language as the possession of a single individual. For Unilingua is not subject to Wittgenstein's arguments against a private language, since it is only a contingently private language – one that is as a matter of fact known to only one individual, whereas Wittgenstein's arguments tell only against the possibility of an *essentially* private language – one that *could* not be known to more than one individual.

This retort is too swift. The objection was not against the very notion of an idiolect, but against treating that notion as primary in a philosophical account of language. For Unilingua (if it existed) would not exist in the void, that is, independently of the existence of other languages, any more than most human languages do: there might be, or might once have been, languages of remote forest tribes of which this was true, but it would not be true of Unilingua. When, for example, its inventor came to consider Unilinguan place-names, all that he would have had to decide is what forms they should take: which particular words the language was to use to denote Germany, Italy, Greece, Rome, Paris, etc. The necessary *background* for the use of those words – the whole institution of the use of place-names – would already be in existence; the use of place-names in Unilingua would depend on and exploit the existing practice of using the corresponding names in other languages. When Quine introduced the notion of radical translation in *Word and Object*, he hit on an important point of which he then lost sight in his retreat to the idiolect: namely that the existence of accepted standard translations between languages is itself a feature of linguistic practice of which account would have to be taken in any complete description of that practice. This fact is exploited in Kripke's 'Puzzle about Belief' – does Pierre believe contradictory propositions? – which depends essentially on the fact that "Londres" is accepted as the equivalent in French of the English name "London".[12] It is not a *hypothesis*, which might be refuted by more careful observation of linguistic behaviour, that they are equivalent: it is a principle which cannot be called into question, since it is constitutive of the uses of the respective place-names in the two languages. The point does not apply to place-names only: it is also constitutive of the significance attaching to public utterances of various kinds – above all, those of politicians, but also those of scientists – that there are standard translations of them into other languages; and a politician must hold himself responsible to the effect of those standard translations of his utterances as much as to the meanings of his words in the language he is using. Hence the true unit for a fully adequate description of linguistic practice would not even be a single language, on the ordinary understanding of the word "language". It would be a maximal set of languages connected by the existence of standard translations between them (that is, of a large fragment of one language into one of the others).

To this it might well be replied that, although a *complete* description of linguistic practice might well require mention of complex social institutions involving the interaction of many people, a first approximation to such a description could content itself with an account of an idiolect. That is all that is required for a notion to be taken as primary: it was acknowledged in advance that the full account would have to build on this notion, explaining the large overlap of idiolects that constitutes a dialect (in that sense of "dialect" in which it means a version of a language, rather than a language without status), and the more restricted overlap that constitutes a language. Indeed, even a description of an idiolect will have to present it as being understood by the speaker as an instrument for communicating with others: forms of greeting, conventional responses to greetings and to polite enquiries, requests, questions, instructions and

---

[12] S. Kripke, 'A Puzzle about Belief', in A. Margalit (ed.), *Meaning and Use*, Dordrecht, 1979.

commands cannot be explained except as designed to be addressed to others. This is made explicit in Davidson's refinement of the notion of an idiolect, namely as the language used (at a given time) by one particular speaker in addressing one particular hearer.

It is perfectly true that, if there were a language that only one person knew, we could learn to understand it in the same way that we can learn any other language, namely by asking that person to teach it to us. Davidson's version of this is that, if we can determine the circumstances in which he holds various sentences of his language, or, rather, various actual or potential utterances of those sentences, to be true, we can construct a theory of meaning for his language just as we should construct one for a language spoken by many people. But this leaves unexplained precisely what needs explanation – the connection between truth and meaning, or, more exactly, between truth-conditions and use. It suggests a certain picture of the employment of language for communication which is overwhelmingly natural, but which is indeed subject to Frege's criticisms of psychologism. Two people are talking together; that is to say, each in turn utters sounds of a certain kind. We know, however, that they are not merely uttering sounds: they are narrating events, asking questions, making conjectures, arguing for certain conclusions, etc. Philosophy of language begins with wonder at this familiar fact: *how*, by simply making certain sounds, can they do these sophisticated things? The most immediately obvious answer is: they are speaking a language they both understand. That is, it is what each has in his head that makes the sounds he utters the bearers of meanings, and enables him to construe those uttered by the other as carriers of meaning. *That* is, fundamentally, the picture suggested by treating the notion of an idiolect as primary: what gives to the expressions of the idiolect the meanings that they have is what is in the head of the individual whose idiolect it is; communication is possible between two individuals when they have the same idiolect, that is, when they have the same thing in their heads. Given a definite conception of a theory of meaning, we can then say what it is that each has in his head that makes his utterances meaningful and enables him to understand the other. For instance, according to Davidson the theory of meaning will lay down what has to hold if something true is to be said by uttering a given sentence in given circumstances. Each participant in the dialogue has such a theory, and these theories coincide, or nearly so; that is what makes their utterances significant and makes it possible for them to understand one another.

That picture is vulnerable, as it stands, to the charge of committing the error of psychologism, however carefully its proponent distinguishes between knowledge of a theory of meaning and a state of consciousness. For if my hearer's understanding of what I say depends on what is in his head, how can I know, save by faith, that he understands me as I intend? It would be no use his trying to tell me what his theory of meaning was: for, if he did, I should still be in doubt whether I understood his explanation of it as he intended; and, in any case, his knowledge of the theory is only implicit knowledge, which he is unable explicitly to formulate. His responses accord with the presumption that his theory of meaning is the same as mine, it may be answered; as *I* understand them, they appear both intelligible and to the point. But might there not be a *subtle* difference between his theory of meaning and mine, which resulted in a persistent but undetected misunderstanding between us? Indeed there might: that actually happens sometimes. Such a misunderstanding might not come to light: but it is essential that it *could* come to light, and indeed that it would do so if we pursued the topic of discussion sufficiently far. That is what saves this account from the mistake committed by psychologistic theories.

It saves itself only by issuing a promissory note, however. We need to be told by what means I can recognise the other speaker as having the same theory of meaning as I do: that is, what use one who assigns certain truth-conditions to the sentences of a language will make of those sentences. All talk in this connection of discerning a speaker's intentions is mere gesturing in the desired direction, until that connection between truth and meaning – and hence between truth-conditions and linguistic practice – which we were presumed to know has been made explicit to us. Only when it has been shall we be able to see whether the truth-theory is superfluous or not. For the connection, once explained, will show how possession of the truth-theory issues in a disposition to make certain assertions in certain circumstances, to respond to the assertions of others in certain ways, and, doubtless, to ask certain questions, manifest certain doubts, and so on. The question will then be whether such a complex disposition could not have been described directly, rather than by a detour through the truth-theory. The answer is far from obvious in advance. But, so long as the connection remains unexplained, the account gains its persuasive force illegiti-mately, through an appeal to the illicit picture of meaning and understanding as depending on private and incommunicable knowledge of a theory informing a speaker's utterances and his perception of the utterances of others.

All this applies, of course, as much to a theory of meaning for a common language as it does to one intended to apply to an idiolect: in the former case, too, it is not enough to provide a theory of truth – an equivalent of Frege's theory of *Bedeutung*: the connection of the truth-conditions so specified with actual linguistic practice must be explicitly displayed by the theory. But when the idiolect is taken as primary, we naturally see its basic function as being that of a vehicle of thought: an *idiolect* is not naturally regarded as, in the first instance, an instrument of communication. There is then a stronger, indeed almost inescapable, temptation to regard an inner state of the individual concerned as being that which confers on the expressions of the idiolect the meanings that they bear. This inner state is his mastery of the idiolect, naturally conceived in this context as consisting in his implicit knowledge of a theory of meaning for it. It is this, on such a conception, that constitutes his attaching those meanings to the expressions, and which therefore also constitutes their *having* those meanings: they mean what they do because he understands them as he does. When the theory of meaning is taken as applying to a common language, on the other hand, that language is more naturally thought of as primarily an instrument of communication: it therefore becomes much easier to regard the significance of expressions of the language as due, not to any inner states of the speakers, but to the practice of employing the language, that is, to what the speakers can be observed to say and do. The significance of a chess move derives from the rules of the game, and not from the players' knowledge of those rules. They must, of course, know the rules if they are to play; but we can explain the significance of a move by reference to the rules alone, without having to explain in what the players' knowledge of them consists.

(viii) Meaning and understanding: theoretical and practical abilities

I have stated several times in the past that a theory of meaning is a theory of understanding;[13] but I now think that the relation between the two concepts is more subtle than I formerly supposed. There is, indeed, much to be said in favour of the view that the two concepts are correlative, and that neither can be explained without the other. Chess may be said to have rules only in virtue of the players' knowing them and following them. In human play, there is a distinction between rules of the game and accidental regularities: and there are many accidental regularities – legal moves that no one makes because they would obviously be bad, and other moves which would in fact be good but which everyone has overlooked. If chess were merely a natural phenomenon, on the other hand, the movements of the pieces being made by unintelligent or even inanimate creatures, it would not be a *game* and would not have *rules*. There would, of course, be observable regularities in the moves; but there would be no sense to the distinction between rules and regularities. Likewise, it is

[13] For example in 'What is a Theory of Meaning?', in S. Guttenplan (ed.), *Mind and Language*, Oxford, 1975, p. 99: to be reprinted in M. Dummett, *The Seas of Language*, Oxford, forthcoming 1993.

essential both to our use of language and to any faithful account of the phenomenon of human language that it is a rational activity, and that we ascribe motives and intentions to speakers. In any linguistic interchange, we are concerned to discern such intentions: to understand why a speaker said what he did at a particular stage, why he expressed it in that particular way, whether he meant it ironically or straightforwardly, whether he was changing the subject or, if not, why he thought it relevant – in general, what his point was or what he was getting at. This estimation of speakers' intentions is not, of itself, peculiar to the particular language, or even to language as such: it proceeds according to the ordinary means we have for estimating the intentions underlying people's actions, non-linguistic as well as linguistic. But it is based upon what we know or presume about the speaker's knowledge of the language: we shall make different estimates according as we take him to be educated or uneducated, a native speaker or a foreigner, and so on. It is only because he knows the language – the meanings of the words, the various possible constructions, and the like – that we can ascribe to him motives and intentions in speaking; and so it is only because speakers consciously understand the words they use that linguistic exchange has the character that it has.

Various alternative possibilities point up the force of saying that speakers *consciously* understand how their sentences are composed of words and what those words mean. We can imagine engaging in a language-like process of exchanging information, but unconscious of the means employed: I here side-step the question in what medium we should store the information so communicated, but I assume that we are conscious of having it. We could, then, recognise that another was speaking, as one does when one hears someone talking next door without being able to discern the words; and we could recognise that we ourselves were replying; but in neither case could we articulate or reproduce the utterances. At the end of an exchange, each participant would be in possession of new information, without knowing in detail how it had been conveyed, or how he himself had transmitted information. We may suppose that there were different 'languages', and that a training – quite unlike the language-learning we go through – was necessary to acquire one: but none of us would *know* the language in which he had been trained. In such imaginary circumstances, we could enquire why someone had conveyed such-and-such information to us, but the intentions we ascribed to others would be limited by the constraints on their consciousness of the means used: we could not, for example, ask why someone had expressed himself in one way rather than another, not only because we should not be aware that he had, but because, even if we were, *he* would not have been. Other similar fantasies will illustrate by contrast other respects in which our use of language is (normally) a fully conscious activity.

The basic reason for considering meaning and understanding to be correlative concepts is, of course, that the meaning of an expression is what someone has to know if he is to understand it. This relation between them constrains admissible characterisations of meaning: it must be represented as something that a speaker *can* know. Thus far, then, the connection between the concepts is straightforward and undeniable; but we run into deep waters as soon as we ask in what sense the word "know" is used in the phrase "know the meaning". For, on the one hand, it is, as we have seen, *conscious* knowledge; and, on the other, it cannot in all cases be explicit, verbalisable knowledge, if only because it would be circular to explain someone's understanding of the words of his language as consisting, in every case, in an ability to define them verbally.

Nor is it mere practical knowledge, like knowing how to swim or to skate. I once described a theory of meaning for a language as 'a theoretical representation of a practical ability':[14] the idea was that we can describe the articulation of this highly complex practical ability – the ability to speak a particular language – by representing it as a possible object of

[14] See 'What is a Theory of Meaning? (II)', in G. Evans and J. McDowell (eds.), *Truth and Meaning*, Oxford, 1976, p. 69: to be reprinted in M. Dummett, *The Seas of Language*, Oxford, forthcoming 1993.

propositional knowledge, while acknowledging that it is in fact not propositional or theoretical, but practical, knowledge. The idea is not absurd in itself: in describing a complex ability, for instance that of playing a musical instrument, we may need to enunciate some propositions as a preparation for saying what that ability involves doing. But, as an explanation of what it is to understand a language, it will not work, because the ability to speak a language is not a straightforward practical ability. We speak of "knowing how to swim" because swimming is a skill that must be learned; if some of us were able, like dogs, to swim the first time we found ourselves in the water, it would make perfectly good sense for someone to say that he did not know whether he could swim or not, never having tried. But it makes no sense for anyone to say, as does a character in one of P. G. Wodehouse's novels, that she does not know whether she can speak Spanish or not, since she has never tried. Someone who cannot swim may know quite well what swimming is, so as to be able to tell whether someone else is swimming: but someone who does not know Spanish also does not know what it is to speak Spanish, and can be fooled into thinking that someone is doing so when he is only uttering Spanish-sounding nonsense words. An ability which it is necessary to have in order to know what it is an ability to do is not a straightforward practical ability: it involves knowledge in some more serious sense than that in which we speak of knowing how to swim.

Just because the notion of knowing a language is problematic, the relation between a theory of meaning for a language and a speaker's mastery of it is problematic also. There is a strong temptation to equate the speaker's mastery with a knowledge of a correct theory of meaning; but, once the applicability to this case of the notion of a theoretical representation of a practical ability is rejected, the equation can no longer be maintained. Ordinary speakers do not explicitly know, and could not understand, a formulation of a theory of meaning for a natural language: indeed, nobody knows such a thing, because many of the problems of constructing one remain unsolved. Moreover, an attribution of explicit knowledge of such a theory, even if not grossly implausible, would be circular as a general account of the understanding of language, because the theory would have to be formulated in some language understood by the speaker. But falling back on the notion of implicit knowledge will not solve the problem: for knowledge explains an ability only in so far as it *delivers* relevant information at necessary moments; and we have no account of the deliveries of such implicit knowledge or of the means of eliciting them.

It is certainly a philosophical necessity that we should be able to explain what knowledge of a language, and the understanding of expressions of that language, are: it is, moreover, a requirement on a theory of meaning that it allow of such an explanation. But, for all that, a theory of meaning does not need to *use* the notion of understanding: it is enough that it characterises *what* a speaker must know if he is to understand the language, without resolving the difficult problem of the *mode* of that knowledge. Our lack of an adequate account of understanding is fatally damaging to the strategy of taking the notion of an idiolect as primary; but the objectivity of meaning requires that a speaker's understanding of his language must manifest itself in his employment of it, and can contain no elements that cannot be so manifested. A theory of meaning, if it is genuinely to explain the practice of speaking that language, must connect its representation of the meaning of an expression with those ways of employing it or its components by means of which a speaker manifests his understanding of it: and in this manner it will altogether escape both the charge against Davidson's theory that it leaves a lacuna where that connection ought to be, and the objection Frege brought against psychologism. By thus explaining how understanding is manifested, such a theory of meaning will go a long way towards being a theory of understanding also. But I believe it to be a mistake to think that a full account of linguistic understanding has been provided when its manifestations in the use of language have been described, as I understand Wittgenstein to have supposed, for that in effect reduces mastery of a language to possession of a practical ability: and, for the reasons I have explained, I believe it to be more than that, but something exceedingly difficult to describe.

CHAPTER 14

Conclusion: a Methodology or a Subject-Matter?

In discussing the relation of analytical philosophy to some of its forebears, have I not misrepresented the linguistic turn, at least as it has been manifested in the most characteristic productions of that philosophical school? I have concentrated principally on questions involving language in general, how its significance should be explained, what relation it has to thought and what relation thought has to perception: but these are questions of a traditional philosophical kind, even if the fundamental axiom of analytical philosophy prompts untraditional answers to them. The main novelty of analytical philosophy surely was, however, that it eschewed the old questions, and replaced them by new ones relating, not to language in general, but to particular forms of linguistic expression. Thus, in the *Philosophical Investigations* Wittgenstein first says, "We feel as if we had to *see into* phenomena", but then repudiates the feeling, saying, "our investigation is not directed towards *phenomena*"; rather, he says, "We remind ourselves of the *kind of statement* that we make about phenomena".[1] We must not ask, for example, about the phenomenon of sudden understanding, but about the use of statements of the form, "He suddenly understood ... ". But what is the difference? If we can explain what it is for someone suddenly to understand something, have we

[1] L. Wittgenstein, *Philosophical Investigations*, I-90.

not thereby explained what it means to say that he has
suddenly understood it? And, conversely, if we have explained
what it means to say that someone has suddenly understood
something, must we not have said what it is for such a
statement to be true, and hence have explained what sudden
understanding is?

The answer depends on whether Wittgenstein's advice is
tactical or strategic. His intention is to discourage us from
scrutinising instances of sudden understanding in order to
identify some inner experience that constitutes it: for, as he
argues, no inner experience could *be* understanding, since
none could have the consequences of understanding. His
advice is to replace the question, "What is sudden
understanding?", by the question, "How do we use statements
attributing sudden understanding to someone?". This advice
is merely tactical if he supposed that essentially the same
answer would serve for both questions, but thought that we
should be more likely to arrive at the right answer if we
addressed ourselves to the second question than if we pursued
the first: it is strategic if he thought the first question
intrinsically misguided and hence unanswerable. Someone
who treated it as purely tactical could adopt Wittgenstein's
methodology while still holding that the meaning of an
assertoric sentence is to be given by laying down the
conditions under which an utterance of it constitutes a true
statement: for, if that is his model for how meaning is to be
given, he must agree that a correct answer to the question,
"What does a statement attributing sudden understanding
mean?", will immediately yield an answer to the question,
"What *is* sudden understanding?"

Wittgenstein surely did not mean his advice as tactical,
however. Rather, he rejected the conception that the meaning
of a statement is to be given by characterising its
truth-conditions, and treated truth as an essentially shallow
concept, to be exhaustively explained by appeal to the
equivalence thesis that "It is true that A" is equivalent to "A".
Describing the use of a sentence, as Wittgenstein understood
the matter, consists in saying under what conditions we

should be disposed to utter it, to what criteria we should appeal to decide whether the statement so made was true, what might subsequently compel us to withdraw it, what we commit ourselves to by making such a statement or by accepting it as true when made by another, what we take to be the point of making it or of having that form of words in our language at all, and what responses to a statement of that kind are considered as required or, if none are required, as at least appropriate. That is to say, the use of an expression should be characterised, not in terms of a conception of truth-conditions that *guides* our use, but directly: we have, that is, to describe the actual *use* that we make of the expression – when we employ it, how we respond to another's employment of it; and this must be stated by reference to circumstances that we can recognise as obtaining – for instance, criteria that we can effectively apply. The use so described completely embodies the meaning of the expression: nothing further, concerning what is required for a statement involving that expression to be true, or equivalently, the state of affairs asserted by such a statement to obtain, is required.

Indeed, the very notion of a state of affairs is called in question by this view: when we have stated the consequences that follow from saying that someone suddenly understood, and, more particularly, have described the types of circumstance in which it will be acknowledged as right to say it, and have noted the variety of these circumstances, we shall have been cured of the disposition to invoke an independently conceivable "state of affairs" that renders the statement true: to say that such a state of affairs obtains is just to say that the person in question suddenly understood, and there is no way of coming to know what state of affairs that is save by describing the use of the expression "suddenly understood" in the manner already indicated.

It is thus evident that the methodological principle advocated, and observed, by Wittgenstein is very far from being free of presuppositions. On the contrary, it rests upon a quite definite conception of what meaning consists in and, consequently, how it is to be characterised. But such a conception is not simply to be propounded, as if it had only to be stated to be acknowledged as correct, as Wittgenstein apparently thought: it stands in need of justification. That is immediately clear from the need to distinguish between what is customarily said and what is justifiably said. It is, no doubt, salutary to remind ourselves of the kind of statement we are accustomed to make about phenomena; but our habits require scrutiny. Suppose that we are concerned with the question that occupied us in Chapter 12, whether we can ascribe thoughts to animals. Wittgenstein himself makes relevant comments, such as "We say a dog is afraid his master will beat him, but not, he is afraid he will beat him tomorrow",[2] and "A dog believes his master is at the door. But can he also believe his master will come the day after tomorrow"?[3] No doubt Italy is different from England in this respect: but if we were to attend to what people in England actually do say about dogs, we should find that it consisted principally of remarks like, "He understands every word you say." Plainly, such a remark, however frequently made, has no authority: we need to distinguish between what is customarily said and what the conventions governing our use of the language require or entitle us to say. Now, however, it appears rather less a matter of assembling reminders of what everyone knows than Wittgenstein liked to make out: to draw such a distinction requires some theoretical apparatus. More generally, what is proposed is, in effect, an array of notions which together are claimed to suffice to characterise a mastery of a language; and this is proposed in conscious opposition to the conception of meaning as given in terms of truth-conditions advocated by Frege and in the *Tractatus*, and, rightly or wrongly, still exercising a profound influence on the thinking of philosophers. In my own tentative view, it does so wrongly: but strong arguments are needed to establish this. It was argued in the last chapter that much needs to be said to show a truth-conditional theory of meaning to yield a satisfactory account of how a language functions – far more than Davidson

[2] Ibid., I-650.
[3] Ibid., II (i), p. 489.

believes it necessary to say, and more than anybody has succeeded in saying: and, at that, I did not adduce my principal reasons for doubting that the approach in terms of truth-conditions is the right one. But there are, on the face of it, equally strong objections to the approach in terms of use favoured by Wittgenstein: these objections need to be met, not just ignored. By displaying a hostility to systematic theories, a follower of Wittgenstein may evade them: but this cannot alter the fact that he is employing a methodology which rests on general ideas about meaning, and that these general ideas can be vindicated only by a plausible sketch of a systematic account of a language in terms of just those ideas.

No one capable of recognising profound philosophy can open the *Philosophical Investigations* without perceiving that it is a work of genius. The technique it employs is, however, based upon a quite particular conception of what meaning consists in, a conception consciously held. Indeed, any enquiry that proceeds by means of linguistic investigations must be founded, consciously or unconsciously, on some such conception, which will be revealed by whatever is treated as being an adequate account of the meaning of expressions. We have no business to accept or reject any such conception as a matter of personal taste. Especially for those who still adhere to the fundamental axiom of analytical philosophy, it is a crucial matter to decide on the correct model for meaning and understanding; and only an explicit enquiry into the correct form of a theory of meaning for a language can decide the question.

Appendix

Interview

The following is the text, as published in the original German edition of this book, of an interview with me conducted by the translator, Dr Joachim Schulte, on 31 October 1987. A published interview is a joint production. The interviewer selects the questions, guides the course of the interview, rearranges it in a more natural sequence, suppresses irrelevant or ill-considered answers, and changes what is clumsily into what is elegantly expressed; he is quite as much responsible for the eventual text as the person interviewed. For this reason, I have kept the text as close as possible to that printed in the German edition. Two of my answers I could not resist the temptation to improve, but I have been careful to avoid so changing them as to affect Dr Schulte's subsequent questions.

*

SCHULTE: In recent years many laments have come out of Britain over the academic situation of the universities. Their grants have been cut, departments of philosophy have been closed: the position is bleak. Let us talk about the past: how was it forty years ago in Oxford? Did you not have the feeling then that really important developments were taking place in philosophy, that something decisive was happening?

DUMMETT: Things looked so utterly different then. I was an

undergraduate from 1947-50 – just after the War – and there was tremendous self-confidence and tremendous insularity. Most philosophers in this university at that time were convinced that all interesting work in philosophy was being done in Oxford. They were amazingly complacent about that. They certainly thought that nothing very valuable was being done in America, and still less on the continent of Europe. Wittgenstein was still teaching at the time – at Cambridge. A few people in Oxford knew something of what he was teaching; the rest wondered – they all knew that it was very important, but they weren't sure what it was. But, Cambridge apart, everything worthwhile in philosophy was happening in Oxford. There really was enormous self-confidence; we know how to go about things in philosophy, they thought; we know how to pose questions and how to set about answering them.

I myself felt out of sympathy with all that. Ryle's *The Concept of Mind*, when it came out, made *the* basis for discussion for quite a long time: it was quite difficult to get away from it. I did not think that Ryle's positive influence was so great: his negative influence, in teaching us to disregard so many things – Carnap, for example – was much greater. I felt quite hostile to Austin's influence. I thought he was a very clever man, but I felt his influence on philosophy to be noxious. I therefore felt aloof from much of this, and certainly no part of any great movement taking place in Oxford.

I was very sceptical about Oxford's complacency. Quine's first visit to Oxford, which took place in the early '50s, caused me some amusement. He was then in his forties – not the grand old man that he is now. It was entertaining to watch many Oxford philosophers, who had a tremendous urge to engage in combat with him and took it for granted that they were going to win; since they had not troubled to read what he had written and were unaware of the subtlety of his position and his skill in defending himself, they were extremely chagrined when each time they lost. Austin was the only one who took the measure of Quine. There was a meeting of the Philosophical Society at which Austin read a paper and Quine replied. Austin's paper was a criticism of some tiny footnote to one of Quine's papers – a very small point indeed. Austin obviously knew what he was up against; he was the only one to do so.

I saw a great deal of Quine whilst he was in Oxford and had many discussions with him. I was not completely sympathetic to his views, but I felt much more sympathetic to them than anyone else in Oxford.

Of course by then we did know what Wittgenstein had taught: the *Philosophical Investigations* had been published, and a little before that the *Blue Book* and the *Brown Book* had arrived in typescript and been read by everyone. I was deeply impressed, and for some time regarded myself, no doubt wrongly, as a Wittgensteinian. I had of course also a great interest in Frege.

SCHULTE: Was it an interest from the very start of your philosophical studies?

DUMMETT: Not from the very start. It just so happened that Austin did a very good thing by inventing an optional paper in P.P.E., which I read, which was called, absurdly, 'Foundations of Modern Epistemology', and consisted of a number of set texts, starting with the *Theaetetus*, and finishing with Frege's *Grundlagen*. It was for that purpose that Austin translated the *Grundlagen*. I read that book because I had chosen to take that paper. I was absolutely bowled over by it; I had never read anything of that quality in my entire life. I therefore decided that I had to read everything that this man had written. Very little of it was in English then, and my German was very rudimentary at that time, so I sat with these texts and a dictionary. I thought Frege's work was absolutely masterly. It was from it that I acquired an interest in mathematical logic and in mathematics itself. After I was elected a Fellow of All Souls I worked on my own on mathematics for a year from books, and then I took tutorials for a year to learn some more. It was really Frege who pointed me in that direction, and I have never lost my interest in him. Of course when I started reading philosophy as an undergraduate I did not know who Frege was. His was just one of those names that occurred in the *Tractatus*, like that of Mauthner.

SCHULTE: So you owe something to Austin after all?

DUMMETT: Yes, of course I do. I do not want to appear completely hostile toward Austin, but I do believe that his influence on philosophy – as opposed to his writings – was harmful and pushed people in the wrong direction.

SCHULTE: Do you think that the label "Oxford Philosophy" is a descriptively correct one at least? Do you think it was ever right to have a label covering both Austin and Ryle, who were very different, and all the young men of the time ...?

DUMMETT: I think it was a fair enough label. There were sufficient similarities, and most of them thought of themselves as belonging to a single school. There were a few people, myself included, who didn't want to be identified with this school. Elizabeth Anscombe, needless to say, was one and Philippa Foot another. What is difficult to remember now is that this high valuation which Oxford philosophy placed upon itself was generally accepted in most parts of the United States. Austin, for example, went to Berkeley to give lectures; they were enormously impressed with him there and tried desperately to induce him to join their department. There were many people in America, now in their late 50s or early 60s, who were really fired by the work of members of the Oxford school, far more than by Wittgenstein's. Except by Kripke, Malcolm, Allbritton, Dreben and a few others, very little attention is paid to Wittgenstein in the United States. That is one big difference between American and British philosophy. Maybe we do not understand Wittgenstein aright, but at least we try to.

*

SCHULTE: In the book you repeatedly call Frege the grandfather of analytic philosophy. Do you think there is anyone else who might have a claim to that label, or is he the only grandfather?

DUMMETT: He's the only grandfather, I think – though I know one normally has two grandfathers. Russell and Moore seem to me more like uncles, or possibly great-uncles. I suppose you would have to call Bolzano a great-grandfather. In Bolzano there is the same rejection of the psychological approach that one finds in Frege, but not the richness of the semantic analysis.

SCHULTE: The complaint is made about your writing on Frege that while you have developed certain fruitful aspects of his work, you have very often read more into it than is really there, that your interpretation is not historically sound. Even if those critics were right, would you think that bad?

DUMMETT: They are partly right about my first book, *Frege: Philosophy of Language*; but it was not altogether a bad thing. I don't accept that I read too much into Frege's work: I don't think that's true. But I do now regret that I wrote that book so unhistorically. I thought that the interesting links are between Frege and what comes after, and not between Frege and what came before; and I still think so. But this led me deliberately to write the book in a particular manner, which I now regret.

This shows in the absence from the first edition of almost all references. I inserted them in the second edition; but it goes deeper than that: it concerns the manner of composition. I adopted it because I found it a distraction to thumb through and locate the passage I had in mind. I was wanting to think about and discuss the topic, and I found from experience that it slowed me up to search for the references: I therefore decided to put them in later, and then, idiotically, forgot to do so.

This, however, would have had a bad effect even if I had

remembered. It is much better to cite the actual passage, even at the cost of a longer discussion. One effect of quoting from memory without looking up the passage is that you overlook the context and thereby connections that the author makes and that ought to be pointed out and discussed. The other effect is over-interpretation: in some cases, though I think not many, I put too much of a gloss on what I was reporting. I don't think the glosses were wrong; nevertheless one ought to distinguish between actual quotation and interpretation, and I often failed to make that distinction sharply.

The second book, *The Interpretation of Frege's Philosophy*, was of course *about* how Frege should be interpreted, and I was therefore compelled to write it quite differently. It is a serious defect of the first book that it does far too little to trace the development of Frege's thought. It was not just that I did too little of this in the book: I had done too little of it in my own thinking. I ran together things that ought to have been kept apart, because Frege said them at different times and from different standpoints. It does seem to me that his work from 1891 to 1906 is a unity and can be treated as such; I do not know of any significant development in that period, in his opinions, his theories or his viewpoint. But after that period, and especially before it, there was very rapid development – you cannot treat either his early or his late period as a unity. But that I said nothing about Lotze does not trouble me in the least. I shouldn't write that book in the same way if I had to write it now, but thank heavens I don't have to.

SCHULTE: It is noticeable that nowadays Frege's *Nachlass* gets quoted more than the work Frege actually published. Is this not a somewhat unfortunate development?

DUMMETT: The observation is just, but I'm not sure about the reason for it. The published work clearly has greater authority – obviously it does over something he decided not to publish. The only writings that have equal authority are those he unsuccessfully submitted for publication.

SCHULTE: Like 'Booles rechnende Logik und die Begriffsschrift'?

DUMMETT: Yes. There are certain things that are made more
explicit in the unpublished works. The most notable example
concerns the question whether for an incomplete expression
the distinction between sense and reference can still be made.
That it can is stated absolutely clearly in the 'Einleitung in die
Logik' of 1906. But there are many things that are discussed
in much more detail in the *Nachlass*, for instance what logic
is, and the concept of truth; apart from 'Der Gedanke', there's
much more about truth in the unpublished works. It leads one
to wonder what would have happened had the whole *Nachlass*
survived.

*

SCHULTE: We've mentioned Wittgenstein and you said that he
was a very strong influence. You have already said that the
publication of the *Investigations* made a strong impression on
you. What did you think when the *Remarks on the
Foundations of Mathematics* came out later? Perhaps you had
already seen the lecture notes on mathematics.

DUMMETT: I had seen the lecture notes; in Bosanquet's
version, they had been circulated in typescript form at the
same time as the *Blue* and *Brown Books*. I in fact reviewed the
Remarks on the Foundations of Mathematics when it first
came out. I felt simultaneously stimulated and frustrated by
the book. I'll tell you the experience that I had: I had tried to
write this review in the usual way, with the book beside me
and looking up passages in it, and I found that I could not do
it. I couldn't get a grip on Wittgenstein's thought to determine
just what he was saying. When I tried to summarise his views
and quote bits in illustration, I found it all crumbling in my
fingers. So I put the book away and deliberately thought no
more about the review for about three months. Then, with my
now impaired memory of the book, I wrote the review –

deliberately without opening the book again; because then some themes came into sharp focus which I know would grow hazy once more as soon as I opened the book again. Finally, I inserted some references. Although the book made a great impact on me, I felt it to be a far less finished work than the *Investigations* – not merely as a piece of writing, but as a piece of thought.

SCHULTE: In many respects – above all, in the emphasis on constructive features – Wittgenstein's *Remarks on the Foundations of Mathematics* is reminiscent of intuitionism. To other constituents of intuitionist thought he is far less sympathetic.

DUMMETT: There are two main points. First, there is a great divergence between Brouwer and Wittgenstein in their attitude to language. Brouwer keeps saying that a linguistic representation of a proof can be at most imperfect. His attitude is genuinely solipsistic. He really does think it's a matter of what goes on in the mind of the individual mathematician, who cannot perfectly convey to anyone else exactly what it is. Obviously that is utterly contrary to Wittgenstein's ideas on the matter: and not only to Wittgenstein's, but to practically everybody else's. Two things on which surely almost everybody would agree is that mathematics is a communal activity, and that a mathematical proof therefore has to be communicable. There is a strong opposition here between Brouwer and Wittgenstein, and in this matter I sympathise entirely with Wittgenstein. It seems to me that the viability of intuitionism depends on its being able to eliminate that solipsistic orientation which Brouwer bequeathed to it.

The second point is one I find very difficult to accept: Wittgenstein's utter separation of mathematics from philosophy of mathematics. He thought that how mathematicians actually proceed in their proofs is *their* business; it is not for philosophers or anyone else to criticise them, but only to describe what they do. The philosophical reflections of mathematicians on their activity are quite another matter. So the remarks of Wittgenstein that appear constructivist and sympathetic to intuitionism are not meant to have the consequences that Brouwer drew, namely that we have to do mathematics in a different way. I presume that Wittgenstein thought that a mathematician who changed his procedure for philosophical reasons, as Brouwer did, would be committing an error: he ought to keep that part of his thinking completely separate from the purely mathematical part. I have never been able to sympathise with that idea. I do not see why our thought should be partitioned into these various compartments between which no communication is possible.

SCHULTE: How did you first come across intuitionism? Was it a sudden revelation, like the writings of Frege?

DUMMETT: It was a more gradual process. Much I learned for the first time when I became Reader in the Philosophy of Mathematics at Oxford in 1962. I knew something of intuitionism before that: I had written a book I never published called *The Law of Excluded Middle*; I had studied intuitionistic logic, and was interested in the basis on which a law of logic could be criticised or challenged. My article on 'Truth' of 1959 shows a strong influence from intuitionist ideas. But I had studied intuitionistic mathematics very little, and only then began to read all those works of Brouwer that are such heavy going. When I first did so, I was still under the influence of Frege, a more or less unrepentant platonist about mathematics. At first I felt quite hostile towards intuitionism because of its psychologistic tone. But my interest in the question how one can criticise a fundamental law of logic compelled me to study it in some detail and with growing sympathy, as being the only existing theory of a constructivist or verificationist kind that had worked out the consequences for our modes of thinking and of reasoning. Of course I was never sympathetic to the strongly solipsistic or at least idealistic strain in Brouwer's thought. It is extraordinary that, so far as I know, there is not one mention of Frege in the whole of Brouwer's writings. He attacks ideas better represented by Frege than by Hilbert whom he mentions; but it is as if he'd never heard of Frege. If he had known Frege's work, he would have had to reflect what defence to make against his critique of psychologism.

＊

SCHULTE: One of the central questions of many of your writings concerns the form a theory of meaning should take. Now I was wondering, does it matter at all whether we ever construct a theory of meaning of that form which we consider the best one? Otherwise expressed: do we need only considerations bearing exclusively on the form of such a theory, or do we have to have some ideas about the content?

DUMMETT: I think we certainly have to have some ideas concerning the content. I regard the enquiry into the correct form of a theory of meaning, and the whole enquiry into what the theory of meaning should look like, as an instrument of philosophical investigation. Of course there is no possibility of actually constructing a theory of meaning for the whole natural language: that would probably be a useless enterprise, and certainly one beyond our powers to carry out. But a satisfactory account of the form which such a theory would take would answer the fundamental questions of the philosophy of language: what meaning is, and what it is for words and sentences to have the meanings that they do.

I don't think it's possible to restrict oneself to the general form of a theory of meaning because a proposal about the correct form for the theory could not be evaluated until obvious test cases had been tried out – some easy cases to start with but then some difficult ones as well – to see if it was really plausible that a theory of meaning could be given in that way. One would therefore have to pay attention to content even to answer the question about form.

There are, moreover, well-known problems in the philosophy of language which are readily expressed as, or already are, questions about the content of the theory at particular places. The outcome of analyses of modal operators, of adverbs and of ascriptions of belief, for example, could be slotted into and would contribute to a description of those parts of the theory of meaning.

SCHULTE: There has been much talk about giving a theory of meaning for a fragment of a language. Do you think we can really talk of a fragment without having a notion of what the theory of the whole language should look like? Many people say: We know nothing about what the theory for the entire language would look like, but here you have one for this fragment of it. Do you think that this is a fruitful enterprise?

DUMMETT: I think there are two quite different motivations for talking about a fragment. One springs from Tarski's strictures on a semantically closed language. If we try to frame, in English or in German, the outlines of a theory of meaning for a natural language, we have to maintain some notional distinction between the object-language and the metalanguage in which the theory is framed, for we know in advance that there will be the devil to pay if we try to give a theory covering all those semantic concepts used in the theory itself. So for that reason we must distinguish the metalanguage from the object-language, and hence must frame our theory of meaning for what would properly be a fragment of English or of German excluding the semantic terms used in the theory. That is quite a different motivation from that for giving a theory of meaning for some very restricted fragment. To do so is not useless, but it is not clear that success really points the way to the theory's being extended to the whole language. It may very well be that the parts we have left out would force us to construct a very different theory. So, though it's not useless, you cannot build too much on it.

SCHULTE: Is it that the restricted fragment could perhaps serve some other purpose, but not that of answering the philosophical questions concerning the concept of meaning?

DUMMETT: No, the conclusion is the same, the evidence much shakier. Constructing a theory of meaning is not a scientific enterprise, but within science the same thing arises: you may be able to construct a succesful theory for a special case, and you hope that it can be extended to the general case, but you cannot count on it for sure. It may be that when you try to extend it you have to recast the whole theory. I think it is exactly similar in our case.

SCHULTE: A speculative question: Frege spoke sometimes of an 'ideal' language. Do you think that he had in mind a very large fragment capable of being constructed, or was he thinking of a pure ideal that we should strive for but can never actually reach?

DUMMETT: I think there were two conceptions that he did not expressly distinguish. One was that of a language that should represent our thoughts perfectly; this is an unattainable ideal, and I think he knew it to be. For instance, such a language could express any one thought in only one way. Frege believed that corresponding sentences of the forms "A and B" and "B and A" expressed the very same thought; an ideal language, therefore, would not have those two ways of writing it. In other words, a commutative binary operator would have two indistinguishable argument-places: a practical impossibility for any script resembling those we have.

A less demanding condition on an artificial language, often mentioned by Frege, is that it be perfectly equipped for the carrying out of deductive arguments without the risk of fallacy. This he believed to be practicable, and in fact to have been achieved by his logical symbolism. It requires the excision of expressions, including demonstratives and indexicals, defective or unsuitable in various ways.

SCHULTE: So it would have essentially been a means to avoid ambiguities, vagueness, singular terms lacking a reference and so forth?

DUMMETT: Quite so. There would be an absolutely sharp criterion for the validity of an inference; in order to apply it, one must be able to avoid all indefiniteness of truth-value.

SCHULTE: Do you think that what Geach once called 'Hollywood semantics' goes any way in the direction Frege had in mind?

DUMMETT: What did he mean – Montague grammar?

SCHULTE: Yes.

DUMMETT: No: the aims are different. Montague was wishing to construct a syntax and semantics for natural languages as they are. Frege aimed at creating an artificial language free of what he regarded as the many defects of natural language, and hence a reliable instrument for carrying out deductive inferences. It is no coincidence that his solution of the problem that had for centuries baffled logicians, of attaining a *general* analysis of expressions of generality, was achieved by introducing the device of quantifiers and variables that bears no direct relation to the means of expressing generality in natural language. He was not interested in any precise account of the mechanisms of natural language, and was sceptical about the very possibility of one.

*

SCHULTE: In your writings the speech act of asserting plays a central role. If so, there must be some way of distinguishing it from different speech acts, such as questions, commands, etc. The objection has often been made to this that assertoric sentences are used to perform all possible speech acts: we use them to give orders, to make requests and so on. Do you think that it is genuinely important to demarcate the speech act of assertion from others, and do you think that the objection that I mentioned carries weight?

DUMMETT: I certainly think that assertion stands on a different level from the rest, in the following sense. Of many of the other types of speech act, it is relatively easy to give an account, given that you already know what assertion is. Asking a question is a very clear case. Admittedly, there are still problems, for example about how many different types of speech act one ought to allow. With sentences in the imperative mood it's obviously wrong to say that they all serve to give commands; there are also pieces of advice and instructions, such as the instruction on a tin, "Heat the contents slowly". That is indeed in the imperative, but is far from expressing a command. There is a problem here, in my view, since one should not be too precise about what constitutes a command. If someone shouts, "Get off those flower beds!" or "Leave that dog alone!", it is dubious whether that is a command A clearer case is the cry, "Look out!", when someone is about to step in front of an oncoming car. Is that a command? No, it would be wrong to speak in this case of a command.

SCHULTE: A warning, perhaps.

DUMMETT: Yes, a warning.

SCHULTE: But perhaps one does not want to have a special speech act of warning.

DUMMETT: That is where the difficulty lies. Austin takes as the basic question, "How many different things can one be said to do by uttering some sentence or phrase?". He then proceeds to list all those verbs that express an action that may be performed by uttering certain words, and considers that to each of them corresponds a type of illocutionary force. But that is not the right question to ask in this connection. The right question is, "What forms of speech act do you have to know about in order to understand an instance of them? Which practices must you have learned?". I do not think that it is necessary to learn specifically what warnings are in order to give or understand what someone means when he says, "Look out!". So giving a warning should not be considered a type of speech act, parallel to, say, making a request.

Thus I am not saying that there are no problems concerning speech acts of these other kinds. Nevertheless, it is obviously relatively unproblematic to describe the practices involved in performing speech acts of these kinds. By contrast, it is clearly extremely difficult to describe the linguistic practice of assertion. Assertion gains its central importance through its connection with truth. Frege said that sense is closely connected with truth; but truth is likewise connected with assertion or with judgement (according as we concern ourselves with speech or with thought). One cannot know what truth and falsity are unless one knows the significance of assertoric utterances: there is otherwise no basis for distinguishing truth from falsity. In my view, therefore, *assertion* is both a much more difficult concept than *question*, *command* and the rest, and far more fundamental.

Now as for the second part of your question, I'm not very impressed by this objection. Many of the cases that are cited, by Davidson for example, are simply spurious. One has to distinguish between what someone is driving at in saying so and so, and what he is saying. An indicative or declarative sentence that is *genuinely* being used to give a command is one that doesn't admit, except as a very bad joke, a response as if it were an assertion. Many of the examples given are ones in which what the speaker actually did was to make an assertion, although the obvious point behind it was to get the hearer to do something. Such an utterance could certainly not be equated with a command, because a response as to an assertion, while perhaps irritating, would not be linguistically inappropriate. So I don't think it is a very serious difficulty.

SCHULTE: In answering this Davidsonian objection, one has always to bring into play two concepts, namely that of the content of the utterance and that of the point of what is said. Do you think there is any way of achieving a clearer formulation of these two central notions, or is it perhaps important that they remain so loose and open-textured?

DUMMETT: There may be many cases in which the application is difficult, but the principle of the distinction is quite clear. Even to understand one another we have constantly to assess the motives or the intentions lying behind what is said; sometimes this is perfectly obvious and sometimes it's difficult. "Is he saying that as a joke or is he serious?". "Did he think his remark relevant to the previous conversation, or was he changing the subject?". We need constantly, in the course of conversation, to ask ourselves questions of this kind.

It is essential that linguistic utterances are in general voluntary, rational actions and that we have to assess them as such. But the salient point is that such assessments are like those of any non-linguistic action, as when we ask ourselves, "Why did he do that?", or "What was he aiming at in doing that?" One does not have, as it were, to *learn* that as part of acquiring the language. One simply picks it up in the course of learning how to respond to other people and interact with other people.

What should be recognised as a part of the 'language-game', as belonging to our linguistic practice and described within the meaning-theory, is anything that is specific to learning language. There are many things which remain the same from one language to another, but nevertheless have to be learned as part of acquiring language. That seems to me the principal distinction; but I do not pretend that it's always easy to apply. Davidson's idea is that everything that Frege called 'force' can be assigned to the first category, namely of that which is not proper to language as such. It is enough to know the truth-conditions of utterances; apprehending that what was said served to get the hearer to do something or to ask him a question would then be part of assessing the speaker's motives in saying something with those truth-conditions. I simply do not believe that theory.

SCHULTE: We seem always to be in a position to redescribe utterances in such a way that their point becomes clear. But as soon as we try to systematise our means of doing this, difficulties arise; we always come back to reformulating the utterance so as to make the point of it clear.

DUMMETT: I'm not so sure about that. It is often a matter of how one utterance bears on others. "Did he say that as an argument for what he had previously said or as a concession?", we may ask. The answer may not be quite clear. That he's maintaining some thesis but allowing an exception to it may be one way of taking it; another way of taking it may be that he is giving a rather obscure reason for accepting the main contention. The same thing applies to understanding a speech, as opposed to a single sentence. When someone makes a political speech, delivers a lecture or simply speaks at length in the course of conversation, one has to grasp how the various statements that he makes are intended by him to be related to one another. Sometimes he gives an argument for what he has just said, sometimes he gives one for something he is about to say, sometimes he gives an illustration of a general thesis, sometimes he makes a concession or proviso, sometimes he begins a fresh topic. To understand the speech one has to understand at each stage which of these he is doing. The speaker may provide linguistic clues. There are highly formalised ones like "therefore", "for" (as a conjunction), "it has to be admitted that" and "for example"; but their use is not required.

In the absence of such a linguistic indication, this is a matter of discerning the intention or the point of the successive utterances making up the speech. We are not here concerned to distinguish different speech acts, which have to do with the force with which a single sentence is uttered. In the course of a lecture, for example, the lecturer may ask questions which he's going to answer or which he leaves the audience to answer, or may make exhortations such as "Never forget that" or "Don't let yourself be deceived". Even a lecture isn't a series of assertions; but grasping whether something the lecturer says is an assertion or a question is quite different from apprehending its relation to the other things he has said.

*

SCHULTE: You once said that Frege brought about a virtual revolution in philosophy. By his work the primacy held since Descartes by the theory of knowledge was challenged, and the philosophy of language took its place. This thesis has been much discussed and strongly opposed. Would you say just the same today, or would you like to qualify it a little now?

DUMMETT: I don't want to qualify it to any great extent. What I said was perhaps a more accurate description of what happened from Frege onwards than of philosophy before him. One can distinguish the philosophy of language and the philosophy of thought. Frege increasingly tended to say, "What I really talk about is thought and not language", especially after 1906 when he came to believe that language had misled him into constructing the wrong logical basis for arithmetic. He did indeed give a philosophical account of thoughts, in his sense of the term, namely the contents of propositional attitudes: what can be believed, known or doubted. But despite his disclaimers, he did so entirely by means of a sketch of a theory of meaning for language, explaining what it is for linguistic expressions to have senses.

The two projects might be separated, however. One could undertake to construct a philosophy of thought – that is, an analysis of what it is to grasp a thought, to judge it to be true, to have a belief with a certain content and so on – which did not proceed in that way, which did not take an analysis of language as the route to an analysis of thought. Some recent philosophers historically in the analytic tradition, like Gareth Evans and quite recently Christopher Peacocke, have attempted to do exactly that – to explain thought independently of language, and language in turn in terms of notions relating to thought taken as prior in the order of explanation.

From such a standpoint, the philosophy of thought should still be seen as fundamental to the rest of philosophy, though no longer identified with the philosophy of language. That is not to say that the foundations must be completed before anything else can be touched; it remains that the foundation of the subject is an adequate analysis of thoughts, their structure and their relations to one another, and it is on this basis the whole of philosophy will rest. This perspective really was new with Frege, in my view, and it was due in part to his having been the first person to see at all clearly how one might give such an analysis.

Admittedly there had been some attempts by previous philosophers, but they were of little use; no one could take them for a foundation for anything, and they were entangled with epistemology. Frege made a very clear distinction between questions about the content of thoughts and the meaning of sentences, on the one hand, and genuinely epistemological questions about, say, the process of thinking, on the other. So I really think this was a new perspective. What I originally said perhaps gave the impression that everybody after Descartes retained an entirely Cartesian conception of the task of philosophy; that would be a mistake. Nevertheless, even with Kant the fundamental emphasis was epistemological; he did not suppose that there was prior work to be done, but plunged straight into epistemological questions. This was in part because he thought that logic was trivial and that there was nothing more to do in the subject. So I still stand, by and large, by what I said.

SCHULTE: You mentioned Evans and his followers. Do you think that the primacy they accord to the philosophy of thought, independent of language, is in any way a reversion to Descartes, or is it a new conception of thought? Can we make a clear distinction between their theories and those of philosophers before Frege?

DUMMETT: Although one might at first think not, there is in fact a sharp distinction. It is not for nothing that these philosophers really are in the analytical tradition, even though they have turned the fundamental principle of the priority, in the order of explanation, of language over thought on its head. There are two differences. First, their focus is not on knowledge as such. It is true that a clean separation from all epistemological questions is probably impossible to achieve. I'm not pretending that all philosophy since Descartes was just a footnote to him, but at least with him there is no ambiguity. When he speaks of clear and distinct ideas, he is not talking about grasping senses, but about knowledge and the recognition of truth. He isn't raising questions about what the propositions mean, what their content is. He usually takes their content as unproblematic; the question he poses is what we have the right to claim to know. That is not at all the starting-point of Evans and his followers. Their starting-point consists of questions like: What is it to grasp these concepts? What is it to have a thought about oneself, about the present moment or about yesterday? What do we express in language by means of demonstratives, and what is it to have the thought corresponding such a sentence as "This table has just fallen over"? I think that this is a very big difference indeed.

The other difference is extremely important, but more difficult to explain. Evans had the idea that there is a much cruder and more fundamental concept than that of knowledge on which philosophers have concentrated so much, namely the concept of information. Information is conveyed by perception, and retained in memory, though also transmitted by means of language. One needs to concentrate on that concept before one approaches that of knowledge in the proper sense. Information is acquired, for example, without one's necessarily having a grasp of the proposition which embodies it; the flow of information operates at a much more basic level than the acquisition and transmission of knowledge. I think that this conception deserves to be explored. It's not one that ever occurred to me before I read Evans, but it is probably fruitful. That also distinguishes this work very sharply from traditional epistemology.

SCHULTE: It is typical of pre-Fregean philosophy that philosophers like Descartes could really worry about the problem how to distinguish between dreaming and waking. I suppose that cannot be problematic for anyone who accords priority to language. How does the matter stand for Evans and similar thinkers?

DUMMETT: Evans was not worried by this problem in its epistemological aspect. He was worried about delusions, rather than dreams, but in a quite different regard: he was not concerned with the epistemological enquiry, "How can we distinguish between delusions and correct perceptions?", but asked, "What is going on when, under the influence of delusion, you have, or take yourself to have, a thought about what you wrongly think you're perceiving?". That's a question which fascinated him – and rightly, in my view; but that is a very different question from that posed by traditional epistemology.

⁎

SCHULTE: The status of the philosophy of language is assessed very variously by different analytical philosophers. Some regard it as part of the philosophy of mind; others say that it is part of the philosophy of action, on the ground that speech is a type of action. A third view is that the philosophy of language is fundamental and that all other branches of philosophy must ultimately reduce to questions in the philosophy of language. Would you accept any of these three positions?

DUMMETT: I should not identify myself absolutely with any of them, but, of course, if I had to choose, then I'd unhesitatingly choose the last. Making the philosophy of thought part of the philosophy of mind seems to me an outright mistake. If this means a theory like Chomsky's, according to which a theory of meaning is really a theory of something very complicated that goes on in the brain, I think that is a completely unphilosophical way of looking at the matter. Philosophy is not concerned with what *enables* us to speak as we do, but what it is for our utterances to have the meanings that they have, and nothing that happens in the brain can explain that. I do not think anything is gained by regarding the philosophy of language as part of the philosophy of action, either. It is of course true that talking is one mode of doing something; that's undoubtedly correct, but it gets you nowhere. The *only* sense I see in it is something we have already talked about, namely that a linguistic utterance is made with some intention or some motive; hence all those considerations that hold generally within the philosophy of action apply. They belong, however, to the background. It is essential to describe language as a conscious activity of rational creatures. If you were giving a description of human language to some Martians who knew nothing about human beings you would have to explain that to them, or they would not know what sort of phenomenon it was. None of that, however, is specific to language; the specific features of language are not explicable in the framework of the general philosophy of action.

*

SCHULTE: If one looks at recent developments in analytical philosophy impartially, one gets the impression of a new naivety. Twenty or thirty years ago explanations of modal expressions in terms of possible worlds were strongly criticised and regarded as outmoded. Similarly, with many psychological concepts such as intention: it was generally agreed they are useless save as governed by behavioural criteria. But now for several years possible-worlds semantics has been in fashion, and many free-floating mental concepts are employed as needing no further analysis. Is a good tradition being forgotten?

DUMMETT: This question is not easy to answer. Insights that people once had do get lost. I have been struck by the enormous influence of fashion in philosophy: possible-worlds semantics is an excellent example. Such a fashion seizes almost everyone at a particular moment and they all go haring off after it. I don't think that the vogue for possible-worlds semantics was just a mistake. It occurred because Kripke succeeded in using that apparatus to make some strong points that struck everybody forcibly; most then got themselves into a state of mind in which they could hardly think except in those terms. At an earlier period, the distinction between analytic and synthetic propositions had played a similar role: it had become a basic tool of thought, and so seemed indispensable and unchallengeable. I find it very irritating: people talk glibly now about 'metaphysical necessity', for example, without seeing any need to ask themselves what they mean. Whether philosophy has been more subject to the whims of fashion lately than it was before, I do not know; if it has, I don't know what the explanation is. I agree with you that some things do get completely lost: the ground for distinguishing motive from cause, for example.

※

SCHULTE: Let us now talk about verificationism. Is there a clear distinction between the anti-realism which you have discussed and the verificationism of the Vienna Circle?

DUMMETT: To tell you the truth, I find it difficult to assign a clear, coherent doctrine to the Vienna Circle. The theory is often presented as a mere test for meaningfulness, rather than a theory of what meaning is; it then lacks a foundation. A test for meaningfulness – a mere test for whether a given expression has a meaning – requires as a foundation a theory of what meaning is. But it is difficult to state what that theory of meaning could be; I mean, to give a coherent picture of it. One rigorous interpretation of verificationism its proponents surely didn't intend, for it produces ludicrous results. This is that the meaning of a statement consists in a procedure for deciding its truth or falsity, so that if you do not actually have, at least in principle, such an effective procedure, then the statement has to be meaningless. That yields a much stricter principle of verification than they ever dared to put forward, and its results are absurd; it is far too restrictive.

So what's the next step? The natural next step, though never exactly taken by the positivists, who tried to weaken the verification principle in other ways, is the one that interests me. This is one parallel to the intuitionist move in mathematics, namely to say that to grasp the meaning of a statement is to be able to recognise a verification of it if one is produced, without needing to have a procedure for arriving at one. If you say that, however, it seems to me impossible to maintain classical logic, for well-known reasons: the law of excluded middle can then hold only for those statements which you do know how to verify or to falsify. For other statements it's just open, and you're not in a position to claim a determinate truth-value for them. And yet the members of the Vienna Circle were unshakably convinced that classical logic was correct. That was not just a slip: it was central to their whole conception of logic, and to their talk of tautologies in the manner of the *Tractatus*. I therefore cannot see how their views hang together. I do not regard theirs as a theory I reject; I don't regard it as a coherent theory at all.

The second point about logical positivism is difficult to make precise. No doubt none of them would have expressly asserted this, but nevertheless they wrote as if each sentence could have the meaning it does independently of the rest of the language: that is, we attach a meaning to the sentence by knowing the method of its verification, where the verification is thought of as something itself independent of language. It may be some very complicated sequence of sense-experiences, or any one of a large set of possible sequences of sense-experiences, so that the notion of verification is here being implicitly taken as something involving no linguistic component. No operation with language plays any role in the process, and so the meaning as it were attaches directly to the sentence independently of its being part of the language. The members of the Vienna Circle would surely not have said that the meaning is attached independently of the sentence's being part of the language, but nevertheless that is the picture that is conveyed.

The fundamental fact, on the contrary, is that our understanding of language is the grasp of a system or structure. I do not mean that it is a system in the sense denied by Wittgenstein when he said that a language is not a calculus: I mean the existence of multiple inter-connections, so that the understanding of one sentence will in general depend on the understanding of a great deal else of the language, according to the overt or implicit complexity of the sentence. That means that if you give an account of what is involved in understanding some sentence, which may be in terms of verification, that verification will in general involve some reasoning which is itself carried out in language.

Furthermore, because the philosophers of the Vienna Circle conceived of verification as given in entirely sensory terms, as consisting of sequences of sense-data, they were forced to make a radical distinction between the meanings of empirical sentences and the meanings of mathematical ones. It virtually becomes a pun to call them both 'meaningful'. They have two quite different sorts of meaning. That seems to me quite wrong. Rather, there is a scale: mathematical statements lie at one end of the scale, where the verification consists entirely of a process of reasoning – deductive reasoning at that. There are, perhaps, sentences at the other end of the scale which can be used only as reports of observation. Most sentences, however, lie somewhere in the middle of the scale. That, I think, amounts to a very strong criticism of the philosophers of the Vienna Circle. They failed to take into account the inter-connectedness of language, the dependence of the understanding of one part of the language on the understanding of another, and for that reason they had to make this false dichotomy.

SCHULTE: In various places you have stressed that, however strong the arguments for anti-realism may be, we are by nature disposed to remain realists. Is it perhaps necessary, in order to understand anti-realism correctly, for you to be tempted by realism?

DUMMETT: I think that is true. It was in my article 'Truth' that I came closest to absolutely endorsing an anti-realist view. In general, however, I have tried to avoid doing that. I have tried to remain agnostic between a realist and an anti-realist view, but have urged that the usual justifications of realism are inadequate, and that there is therefore a large problem to be resolved. As I said in my article, 'The Reality of the Past', it is in the temporal case that it becomes most repugnant to adopt an anti-realist view, this is, an anti-realist view of the past. There is a very strong drive to take a realist view, and I by no means want to commit myself to dismissing it as a mere error of the human mind. I do not see how the realist position can be defended against the anti-realist attack, but I should be very happy to be shown how it can. Some people take this whole question very seriously, and I think them right to do so. Others react with indignation, because they feel so strongly convinced of the truth of realism that they dismiss the whole discussion as nonsense. They are quite mistaken, in my view, to brush the question aside, for it is a serious philosophical problem. I find it hard to believe that the arguments against realism are as strong as they give the appearance of being. I should be quite unhappy if I found that I really had to take an anti-realist view of the past; that would be for me a very uncomfortable position. It may be that there is some intermediate standpoint, but I cannot see just what it would be.

*

SCHULTE: In the book, you discuss writers whom you seldom mentioned in your earlier works. You talk about Bolzano, you mention Brentano and you discuss Husserl extensively. I take it that this is a fairly recent interest. How does this very different way of doing philosophy strike you?

DUMMETT: I confess that I do not get the pleasure from reading Husserl that I get from reading Frege. Husserl's writing is wordy, and not so sharply expressed as Frege's. All the same, I do find Husserl interesting. The historical question is interesting, too. If you compare the *Logical Investigations* with Frege, they are not so very far apart. Of course, there are considerable differences, and if you look ahead to the later developments, you see them more clearly. It is nevertheless a very interesting question: How did the traditions that they founded come to diverge so widely? What is there in the work of each, at the time when they were closest, that led to that divergence? It is also interesting to ask about the background to the linguistic turn: What was there before that step was taken which made it so natural to take it?

Bolzano I enjoy reading, although I wonder whether whether anyone has ever read the whole of the *Wissenschaftslehre*. It seems to me a great defect that it is so enormous. I have only read selections, but I enjoy reading Bolzano much more than I enjoy reading Husserl.

SCHULTE: There have been some recent attempts to bridge the gulf between phenomenology and analytical philosophy. Is that a genuinely positive development? Would it not be better, in order to come to grips with the problems, to stress the differences, with the aim of discovering which side was right?

DUMMETT: There is much truth in that. The trouble is that the gulf became so wide that it became extremely difficult to communicate at all across it. I do not mean that one should pretend that philosophy in the two traditions is basically much the same; obviously that would be ridiculous. We can re-establish communication only by going back to the point of divergence. It's no use now shouting across the gulf.

It is obvious that philosophers will never reach agreement. It is a pity, however, if they can no longer talk to one another or understand one another. It is difficult to achieve such understanding, because if you think people are on the wrong track, you may have no great desire to talk with them or to take the trouble to criticise their views. But we have reached a point at which it's as if we're working in different subjects. I am glad that there are now many people, both in Germany and in Italy, who are familiar both with Husserl and with Frege and can relate them to one another.

❊

SCHULTE: You were for some time very active politically, not in party politics, but in the struggle against racism. This was clearly prompted by moral convictions. Do you think that in a wide sense these are connected with your philosophical ideas?

DUMMETT: Only in the very widest sense. When I first became involved in it, I certainly did not see it as springing out of my philosophical work. It might have been different if I had done much work in ethics or political philosophy, but I had not – my work all lay at the other end of the subject. I believe, however, that academics in general, and perhaps philosophers particularly, have a duty to make themselves sensitive to social issues, and, if they see an opportunity for doing anything effective, to do it. This is because they are favoured in a particular way: they have time for reflection and they are more masters of their time than most people are, however busy they may be. I think also that they have a particular responsibility. If you are an intellectual, and particularly if you aim to be a philosopher, and therefore to think about very general questions, then you ought to be capable of responding to urgent general issues, whether the public is ignoring them or has fastened its attention upon them.

It's only in that very general sense, however, that I see any connection. In the situation we were then in in Britain, I saw a possibility for me to do something significant in a sector in which there were very few people taking any such action or even aware what the situation was. I do not think I could have respected myself as a philosopher if I had not undertaken that work: I should have felt that all my engagement with philosophy was a sham. But it's only in that general sense that there was any connection with my philosophical ideas.

SCHULTE: There is a prevalent philosophical tradition that

accords a primacy to practical reason. From the standpoint of this tradition, a philosophy that lacks an ethics – a moral philosophy – as an integral part is gravely incomplete. Is that a thought you can respect, or do you think that it to be false?

DUMMETT: Of course I respect it. It is clearly true, but that does not mean that everybody who works in philosophy has also to work in ethics or even, if challenged, to be in a position to say, "The following is my ethical system". In the nineteenth century, there were all these professors of philosophy in Germany who published a *Logic*, a *Metaphysics* and an *Ethics*, and had then produced a 'system'. In this sense, not everybody who does significant philosophical work has to produce a system. Admittedly Frege was not a professor of philosophy, but of mathematics, but he's a clear example of someone who contributed greatly to philosophy, but not at all to ethics. Indeed I'm not sure that I should have liked his *Ethics* if he'd written one. It is of course true that if anyone has a complete philosophy, it has to include ethics. If what is meant is that ethics is the crown of the entire subject, I am not of that opinion.

SCHULTE: Do you wish to write a book on ethics?

DUMMETT: No.

Index

197